SUPER J...

Beverley Piper is a freelance home economist who started writing about microwave cookery when working as a microwave oven demonstrator; she also presented a BBC series on microwave cookery. She originates recipes for various companies and often presents food for display, demonstrations and photography. She is the author of *Fast and Healthy Family Cooking*, *Beverley Piper's Quick and Easy Healthy Cookery*, *Super Juice* and *The Daily Express Entertaining in a Flash*.

Beverley Piper is married to Malcolm Jarvis and they live in Kent.

Also by Beverley Piper

**Fast and Healthy Family Cooking
Beverley Piper's Quick and Easy Healthy Cookery
Super Juice*
The *Daily Express* Entertaining in a Flash***

* Available from Headline

Super Juice for Slimmers

Beverley Piper

HEADLINE

Copyright © 1994 Beverley Piper (text)
Copyright © 1994 Frances Lloyd (illustrations)

The right of Beverley Piper to be identified as the author of
the Work has been asserted by her in accordance with the
Copyright, Designs and Patents Act 1988.

First published in 1994
by HEADLINE BOOK PUBLISHING

10 9 8 7 6 5 4 3 2 1

All rights reserved. No part of this publication may be
reproduced, stored in a retrieval system, or transmitted,
in any form or by any means without the prior written
permission of the publisher, nor be otherwise circulated
in any form of binding or cover other than that in which
it is published and without a similar condition being
imposed on the subsequent purchaser.

ISBN 0 7472 4573 8

Typeset by Keyboard Services, Luton

Printed and bound in Great Britain by
HarperCollins Manufacturing, Glasgow

HEADLINE BOOK PUBLISHING
A division of Hodder Headline PLC
338 Euston Road
London NW1 3BH

Contents

Introduction	1
Fruit Juices	15
Vegetable Juices	45
Snacks, Starters, Soups and Dressings	75
Stir-fries	107
Main Meals	125
Salads and Vegetable Dishes	153
Desserts	181

Super Juice Diet Plans

Low-fat Diet	213
Sweet Tooth Diet	218
Busy Woman's Diet	225
Vegetarian Diet	231
Super Soup Diet	237
Anti-cellulite Diet	244
De-stress Diet	248
Detoxifying Juice Diet	254
Healthy Kids' Diet	257
Pregnancy Plan	265
Index	273

Introduction

This book shows you how to use invigorating, healthy juice as part of an exciting new slimming programme. It encourages you to re-educate your eating habits by combining fresh juice with wholesome foods. Most people now agree we are what we eat, but everyone needs food as fuel just to keep going. Don't feel guilty about eating – just change your foods to healthier ones to enable you to reach your desired, healthy weight without feeling deprived or hungry. Once this target weight is reached, good eating will allow you to keep your weight stable without yo-yoing up and down the scales for the rest of your life.

Juice freshly made on a juicing machine delivers full flavour and maximum amounts of vitamins and minerals straight into the glass. It's nothing like the rather flat-tasting, commercially produced juice sold in bottles, cans and cartons. Just compare the taste with shop products. Fresh juice has no additives, is not pasteurised and what's more, the goodness in the glass quickly enters your blood stream, giving you an almost immediate super-lift. It is fairly low in calories too, so is an absolute boon to slimmers.

As you use this book you will realise that the key to successful slimming is not constantly feeling hungry. You will be encouraged to eat less fat and more complex carbohydrate foods to fill you up and give energy. Fat is the dieter's enemy; it comes hidden in all sorts of foods such as cakes, biscuits, pastry, peanuts, etc., and all fat (including butter, polyunsaturated margarines, lard, oil – including olive oil – and cream) is very high in calories. Butter, for instance, contains 207 calories per 25g (1oz) and lard contains 250. As a comparison 25g (1oz) boiled carrots yields only 6 calories and 25g (1oz) eating apples is a mere 10 calories.

The recipes and diets in this book are all based on the high fibre principle. You won't be advised to skip meals or to exist on a lettuce leaf. The book works on the theory that weight will be lost if you eat plenty of fibre and carbohydrates such as potatoes, brown rice and wholegrain pasta which are easily burnt off. They'll also give you energy and a great feeling of well being (just ask athletes what they prefer to eat). High fibre foods tend to be low in fat and sustaining so you don't crave food soon after you've eaten. A high fibre diet including plenty of fruit and vegetables will soon become a way of life so you won't need to worry about slimming, just eat what you want of the right foods and your body will maintain its correct weight.

FOOD VALUE

Protein
We all need protein for tissue growth and repair but it is unlikely that you're not getting enough. Protein is often hidden in fat – whole milk, cheese, bacon, red meat, etc. – so always opt for low-fat varieties. Use skimmed milk and low-fat cheeses instead of full-fat varieties, choose diet yoghurts instead of cream, avoid peanuts and select chicken without fatty skin instead of red meats. Try to use protein as a garnish instead of a main portion. A full plate of salad or freshly cooked vegetables, topped with a 50–75g (2–3oz) portion of low-fat protein is sustaining and ideal.

Carbohydrates
We have already learned that some carbohydrates are excellent (wholewheat pasta and rice, wholemeal bread,

potatoes in their skins, etc.). However, don't be confused and think that chocolate cake, doughnuts and biscuits are good – they are all also high in fat and sugar and should be avoided.

Vitamins and Minerals
These tiny nutrients were actually only discovered early in the twentieth century when doctors began to understand their importance in preventing disease. Vitamins are divided into two categories: water-soluble and fat-soluble. Vitamins A, D, E and K are fat-soluble and are stored in the body for future use.

Water-soluble vitamins are needed daily to keep the supply topped up, so we must eat fresh fruit and vegetables every day. B and C are two such vitamins. Minerals are also vitally important as they maintain healthy teeth, bones and hair. They, too, must be taken into the body daily as they are excreted through sweat, urine and faeces.

Healthy fresh fruit and vegetable juice is a wonderful, concentrated source of vitamins and minerals and, as vitamins are now definitely thought to play an important role in the prevention of some cancers, what better way to ensure your supply than to drink freshly prepared fruit and vegetable juices which are fairly low in calories too.

Fat-soluble Vitamins
Vitamin A is also known as beta carotene as the body converts the latter into vitamin A. This great vitamin is found in orange and yellow fruits and vegetables, especially carrots, tomatoes, melons, broccoli, etc. Vitamin A is also known as the eye sight vitamin as it maintains good eye sight and is necessary for a healthy immune system. It is great for healthy skin and helps to ward off cancer.

Vitamin D is important for strong bones and teeth. It is produced by the skin when exposed to sunlight, and is found in carrot juice, tomatoes, yellow fruits and in margarine and butter.

Vitamin E is vital for protection of body cells and is an important aid in the healing of damaged tissue. You will find vitamin E in carrot juice, vegetable oil, egg yolk, nuts, wholegrains and dark green vegetables.

Vitamin K aids blood-clotting and helps fractures to heal. Dark green, leafy vegetables and liver are good sources.

Water-soluble Vitamins

Vitamin B is important for the nervous system and also assists in breaking down carbohydrates into energy. Vitamin B is found in wholegrains, brown rice, brewers' yeast and vegetables.

Vitamin B2 is essential for repair of body tissue and is thought to protect against some cancers. Vitamin B2 is found in green leafy vegetables, cereals and brewers' yeast.

Vitamin B3 is important for a healthy heart and for energy. Find it in leafy greens, wheatgerm, potatoes and wholegrain cereals.

Vitamin B6 is necessary for the nervous system and will help to provide energy. Also good for healthy skin, B6 is found in green beans, avocados, liver, wholegrains, egg yolks and lean meat.

Vitamin B12 is essential for healthy blood and assisting the body to break down fat. Find B12 in liver, kidney, fish, shellfish and eggs.

Vitamin C is necessary for healthy joints and ligaments. It protects gums, fights against colds and flu, and may assist in the fight against cancer. Find it in leafy greens, tomatoes and citrus fruits.

Minerals

Calcium is vitally important for growing bones and teeth, and aids blood clotting. Found in seeds, nuts, milk, cheese, kale, parsley and broccoli. Calcium is a particularly important mineral for girls and young women, as it can help prevent osteoporosis in later years.

Iodine is essential for a healthy thyroid and acts as a natural antiseptic. As minute amounts of iodine are added to table salt, it is unlikely that you would not get sufficient from a normal diet.

Iron is vital for healthy blood and for the transportation of oxygen around the body. Deficiency causes anaemia, and pregnant and menstruating women need plentiful supplies of iron. Red meat is a good source of iron, and it is also found in apricots and leafy greens.

Water is a great cleanser which works closely with fibre to rid the body of impurities. It is essential for healthy skin, hair and eyes. Drink plenty of water, using bottled or filtered if necessary; or, if drinking tap water, always use the cold tap in the kitchen or whichever tap is the closest to where water enters the house so you are not consuming water that has been stagnating in a tank.

EAT A BALANCED DIET

A well balanced diet consists of a wide variety of foods and is therefore neither restrictive nor boring. Follow the guidelines recommended by the World Health Organisation and eat more fibre, less fat (especially saturated fat) and less salt and sugar. In this way you're very likely to lose weight naturally and you are helping to prevent heart attacks, strokes, diabetes and cancer – particularly if you eat plenty of fresh fruits and vegetables with, of course, freshly made concentrated juice.

EXERCISE

This gives you a wonderful, uplifting feeling, improves your circulation, reduces stress and helps burn off calories, so start enjoying it.

The type of exercise you undertake really doesn't matter but do it regularly – at least one 20–30 minute session three times each week. Walking briskly, aerobics in front of the TV, jogging, swimming, tennis, football, badminton, squash, etc., are all excellent, and you'll be surprised how quickly the muscles in your body respond and you start to look better, stand taller and appear firmer and slimmer. Clothes will fit better and you'll soon be winning complimentary comments on your new appearance.

HOW TO USE THIS BOOK

Super Juice for Slimmers is divided into two parts. The first half consists of some 120 recipes, divided into sections. There are plenty of fruit and vegetable juices, with the maximum calorie count given as a guide. Do remember that fruit and vegetables are very good for you and that you are very unlikely to get fat from drinking juice. However, as a rough guide, enjoy three juices every day, selecting one fruit juice and two vegetable juices as the calorie count of vegetable juices is normally lower than that of fruit juice. Enjoy mixing concentrated juice with bottled mineral water, diet tonic water, low calorie lemonade or ginger ale for long refreshing coolers. Try freshly made orange juice topped up with dry champagne for a wonderful Bucks Fizz for a special occasion.

The book continues with recipes that are all made with full flavoured, fresh tasting juice as one of the main ingredients. Speedy snacks; starters and dressings; stir-fries and marinated dishes; main meals; salad and vegetable dishes and desserts are all included. Without bothering about counting calories, select recipes from the various sections for your daily meals. Just stick to the following basic principles and you will find it easy to plan filling and sustaining menus that will help you slim effortlessly.

The end of the book contains ten carefully designed seven-day specific diet plans. If you enjoy following a pre-planned diet for weight reduction, select one of these for the first seven days then use the recipes in the front of the book for your maintenance plan.

SUPER JUICE FOR SLIMMERS BASIC PRINCIPLES
Follow these simple rules for a new slim you.

1. Drink two vegetable juices selected from the vegetable juice section and one fruit juice from the fruit juice section daily. These will provide your body with a boost of vitamins and minerals and give you a great feeling of well-being and vitality. They will also help to fill you up so you won't want high calorie snacks.

2. Always eat a high fibre breakfast. 40g (1½oz) bran flakes, All Bran or Weetabix with 100ml (4 fl oz) skimmed milk is ideal, or have two slices wholemeal toast with two teaspoons low fat spread and a little marmalade or have one portion of the natural muesli recipe on page 77.

3. For lunch select a recipe from the starter and snack section and have one serving, or select one of the vegetable and salad dishes and have one portion but don't worry if you're hungry and eat a little more.

Enjoy a wholemeal roll as well if you wish but try not to have any type of spread with it. Finish lunch with one piece of fresh fruit (but not a banana as these are higher in calories).

4. For your main meal select a recipe from the stir-fry section and have one portion only, or one portion of any of the main meal dishes. Always include the serving suggestion given as part of your meal and if pasta or rice is mentioned, use 50–75g (2–3oz) raw weight of wholemeal varieties. If preferred, select from the snack and starter section or the vegetable and salad section again as these are often quicker to prepare and they're filling too.

5. Eat as many fresh vegetables and salad ingredients as you like without adding any type of fat. Eat two pieces of fruit daily.

6. All desserts contain calories so will add to your daily intake. You may prefer to avoid them or have one piece fresh fruit or one diet yoghurt or fromage frais instead. However, the dessert recipes in this book have been carefully compiled to give you something sweet for special occasions and for when you yearn for a pud, so enjoy one portion now and again without feeling guilty – twice a week is fine.

7. Have one treat during the day if necessary, but make it one piece of fruit, two raw carrots, two sticks of celery, one piece of wholemeal toast with yeast extract spread, freshly made juice or two light digestive biscuits.

8. Each day aim to have 300ml (½ pint) skimmed milk in total (part of this will sometimes be used in recipes).

9. As a golden rule think fibre, not calories. Eat more

fibre and less fat so that the pounds roll away naturally.
10. Weigh yourself once a week first thing in the morning and record your weight and progress, rewarding yourself each time a loss is shown with anything other than a calorific treat! Try a bunch of flowers, a new item of make-up or clothing or a visit to the hairdresser.
11. Remember that to lose weight, you must eat fewer calories than your body burns each day. As this varies from person to person, it really is up to you to get the balance right.

CALORIES

Whether you lose or gain weight or simply remain the same depends on how many calories you consume daily. To lose weight the body needs to use up some of its fat stores as energy so you must take in fewer calories from food. As long as you continue to do this for some time you will lose weight.

If you are a woman with only a few pounds to lose, try and stick to 1,000 calories a day or 7,000 per week if that's easier to cope with; but if you have more than a stone to lose, stick to about 1,300 calories a day. Men should still lose weight on about 1,300 calories daily. As has been stressed throughout this book, it is important to eat healthily and to make sure that your calories come from foods which provide you with the essential nutrients needed daily to keep your body functioning well.

Calorie Count

As a guide, the recipes have been calorie counted to give an approximate result. All the juices actually come out higher than they really are because I have had to count the calories that occur in the *whole* fruit and vegetables. When you juice, quite a few of the calories are obviously left behind in the hopper or pulp store. There are a number of variables that make it extremely difficult to count calories in juice – size and ripeness of fruit, how good the machine is at extracting juice, how much water is present in the fruit and vegetables, etc. – and this is why a *maximum* count has been given. However, feel comforted that you won't be consuming as many calories as the counts suggest.

A NOTE ABOUT JUICING

Fruits and vegetables are now readily available throughout the year as fresh produce arrives from abroad to supplement our own stocks which run out as the season in this country ends. Ensure you buy fresh fruit and veg frequently. They are at their best when they look plump, firm and full of natural colour – they'll be bursting with vitamins and minerals at this time too, but during storage valuable vitamins are quickly lost.

Where possible, juice fruits and vegetables without peeling; just make sure that all produce has been scrubbed clean under cold running water first. The exceptions are citrus fruits such as lemons, limes, grapefruits and oranges which all have tough skins – these do need to be peeled before juicing. With grapes, the green stems may be juiced but any hard brown stems should be removed and discarded before juicing. Mangoes also must be peeled and the central stone removed before juicing.

Certain fruits and vegetables are not suitable for juicing – aubergines, avocados, bananas, blackberries and figs are all difficult for the machine to cope with and should not be juiced. If the juicer starts to sound sluggish when using pineapple or onion, stop and peel the onion or piece of pineapple before processing.

HOW TO USE YOUR CONTINUOUS JUICE EXTRACTOR

With the machine assembled, the fruit and vegetables should be washed and prepared to fit the juicer, normally by slicing roughly. Citrus fruits should be peeled first and pips discarded. Store prepared fruits and vegetables together in a mixing bowl beside the juicer.

With the motor running and the appropriate speed selected according to type of produce to be juiced (if more than one speed is offered), feed the fruit and vegetables through the feed tube of the juicer with a plastic plunger. The juicer extracts the liquid out of the produce by centrifugal force. This juice is instantly filtered and passed through into the jug. The residue of the fruit and veg is deposited in the hopper or pulp store. The hopper only needs to be emptied when full, which means you can juice plenty of produce without emptying it, especially on the larger models (there are several manufacturers who offer juicers in two sizes). Emptying the hopper is quick and easy. I use a plastic spatula to scrape the pulp into the bin. Cleaning is also simple – just take the removable components to the sink to be rinsed with washing-up liquid, using a stiff brush to clean the re-usable filter.

COOKS' NOTES

British standard measuring spoons have been used throughout in the testing of the recipes in this book. It is important to follow either imperial or metric measures within any recipe; don't try to mix weights. A microwave oven with an electrical output of 700W has been used throughout.

Fruit Juices

Tangerine and Sharon Fruit Juice

Serves 2

Sharon fruit is the Israeli version of persimmon. This orange-coloured fruit with a dry looking calyx resembles the tomato in appearance. Sweet flavoured and a good source of vitamins, this is another excellent fruit from the Middle East which can be used through its various stages of ripening. It is available in the UK from beginning November until end February.

Maximum kcals per serving: 80

1 sharon fruit
3 tangerines
1 apple

To serve
ice cubes

1. Slice the sharon fruit to fit the juicer and store in a mixing bowl.
2. Peel and segment the tangerines and add to the bowl.
3. Slice the apple and add to the bowl.
4. With the motor running, juice the sharon fruit with the tangerines and apple. Stir the juice.
5. Divide ice cubes between two tumblers. Top up with the juice and serve immediately.

This recipe makes approximately 300ml (10 fl oz) concentrated juice.

Fruit Sunburst

Serves 1

A delicious summery fruit cocktail which tastes superb and looks very pretty. Add a slice of lime to the glass on serving. This drink is also delicious served in tumblers topped up with ice cold sparkling mineral water or slimline lemonade.

Maximum kcals per serving: 73

1 pink grapefruit
2 large ripe plums
100g (4oz) slice fresh pineapple

1. Peel the grapefruit, removing pith. Slice to fit the juicer, discarding pips. Store in a bowl.
2. Slice the plums to fit the juicer, discarding central stone. Add to bowl.
3. Slice pineapple to fit juicer and add to bowl.
4. With the motor running, juice the fruits in the bowl.
5. Stir juice and serve immediately poured into a glass.

This recipe makes approximately 250ml (8 fl oz) concentrated juice.

Melon, Raspberry and Grape Juice

Serves 2

A particularly low calorie, refreshing drink that's high on taste and seems surprisingly sweet on the palate.

Maximum kcals per serving: 75

175g (6oz) slice Galia melon, with skin and seeds
225g (8oz) raspberries
100g (4oz) seedless black grapes

1. Cut melon into slices that will fit the juicer and store in a bowl.
2. Add raspberries to the bowl.
3. Discard any old brown stems from the grapes and add to the bowl, divided into juiceable bunches.
4. With the motor running, juice the fruit. Stir well.
5. Divide juice between two tumblers and serve immediately.

This recipe makes approximately 350ml (12 fl oz) concentrated juice.

Kiwi, Grape and Melon Juice

Serves 2

Kiwi fruits are an excellent source of vitamin C and melons provide valuable vitamins and minerals in the skin which are all delivered into the juice – just one of the benefits of juicing. Melons are low in calories too, so are a boon for the dieter.

Maximum kcals per serving: 63

150g (5oz) slice cantaloupe melon, with seeds and skin
100g (4oz) seedless grapes, black or white
2 kiwi fruit
1 wedge of lemon, peeled

1. Slice the melon to fit the juicer and store in a bowl.
2. Discard any old brown stems from grapes, then add them to bowl in juiceable bunches.
3. Cut kiwi fruit into wedges to fit juicer and add to bowl with the lemon slice.
4. With the motor running, extract juice from the fruit. Stir well.
5. Divide between two wine glasses and serve immediately.

This recipe makes approximately 300ml (10 fl oz) concentrated juice.

Apple and Orange Juice
Serves 2

A truly refreshing juice with a sherbet flavour. Ideal on its own and wonderful as a long drink after sport – just add diet lemonade and stir before serving with plenty of ice.

Maximum kcals per serving: 100

150g (5oz) Cox's Orange Pippin apple
225g (8oz) Bramley apple
2 × 175g (6oz) oranges (unpeeled weight)

To serve
ice cubes (optional)

1. Cut apples into juiceable pieces and store in a mixing bowl.
2. Peel the oranges, leaving on about half the pith. Slice the oranges into juiceable pieces, discarding pips. Add to the bowl.
3. With the motor running, juice the fruit. Stir juice well.
4. Divide the juice between two glasses, add ice if required, and serve immediately.

This recipe makes approximately 475ml (16 fl oz) concentrated juice.

Orange and Pear Juice
Serves 2

You may like to serve this fairly thick juice topped up with soda water. Pears are a reasonable source of vitamins A and E, and are also rich in potassium. Oranges are rich in vitamin C and provide folate so treat this juice as a tonic – it really will give you a lift and if you're trying to avoid biscuits and sweets, sip this particular juice instead. It will take away the craving for something sweet.

Maximum kcals per serving: **74**

2 × 175g (6oz) ripe Williams pears
2 × 175g (6oz) oranges (unpeeled weight)

To serve
crushed ice

1. Slice the pears to fit the juicer and store in a bowl.
2. Peel the oranges, leaving about half the pith on the orange. Cut in slices to fit the juicer, discarding pips. Add slices to the bowl.
3. With motor running, juice the pears and oranges. Stir juice well.
4. Put crushed ice in two tumblers. Divide juice between the tumblers, pouring it over the ice. Serve immediately.

This recipe makes approximately 325ml (11 fl oz) concentrated juice.

Satsuma and Melon Juice

Serves 2

Melons produce a delicious, energy-giving juice and as the skin and seeds are juiced, all the nutrients they contain are delivered into the glass. Satsumas are an excellent source of vitamins B1 and C, and we all know an apple a day keeps the doctor away.

Maximum kcals per serving: 73

225g (8oz) slice melon, with skin and seeds
3 satsumas
1 eating apple

To serve
ice cubes

1. Cut the melon into slices that will fit the juicer and store in a mixing bowl.
2. Peel and segment the satsumas and add to bowl.
3. Slice the apple to fit the juicer. Add to the bowl.
4. With the motor running, juice the melon with the satsumas and apple. Stir the juice.
5. Divide the ice cubes between two tumblers. Top up with the juice and serve immediately.

This recipe makes approximately 350ml (12 fl oz) concentrated juice.

Blackcurrant and Pineapple Shake

Serves 2

Fresh fruit juice mixed with milk and yoghurt makes a delicious drink which doubles as a breakfast or snack, providing plenty of vitamins, minerals and calcium.

Maximum kcals per serving: 147

100g (4oz) blackcurrants
100g (4oz) slice pineapple
350ml (12 fl oz) ice cold skimmed milk
1 small banana, peeled and sliced
45ml (3 tablespoons) low-fat natural yoghurt
5ml (1 teaspoon) clear honey

1. With the motor running, juice the blackcurrants with the pineapple.
2. Put the juice, milk, banana, yoghurt and honey into the food processor. Process until blended.
3. Serve immediately in tall tumblers.

This recipe makes approximately 700ml (24 fl oz) milk shake.

Pink Grapefruit and Kiwi Juice
Serves 2

Bursting with vitamin C and minerals, this pretty juice acts as a great reviver when you're feeling tired. An excellent breakfast juice.

Maximum kcals per serving: 70

1 large pink grapefruit
1 kiwi fruit, peeled
2 eating apples

To serve
slices of orange

1. Peel and slice the grapefruit to fit the juicer, discarding pips. Store in a mixing bowl beside the juicer.
2. Slice kiwi fruit and apple to fit the juicer. Add to the bowl.
3. With the motor running, extract juice from the fruit.
4. Stir well and divide between two wine glasses.
5. Serve immediately, decorated with the slices of orange.

This recipe makes approximately 275ml (9 fl oz) concentrated juice.

Orange, Lime and Grape Juice

Serves 2

Choose sweet black seedless grapes for this drink which is an excellent juice to start children on. I also remove most of the pith from the oranges if I'm juicing for kids as it tends to make the juice taste slightly bitter.

Maximum kcals per serving: **97**

1 large orange
225g (8oz) seedless black grapes
1 small wedge lime, peeled

To serve
crushed ice
mineral water or low-calorie lemonade

1. Peel the orange, removing most of the pith. Cut into slices to fit the juicer, discarding pips. Store in a mixing bowl beside the juicer.
2. Remove any brown woody stems from the grapes, then cut them into bunches to fit the juicer. Add to the bowl with the lime.
3. With the motor running, juice the orange with the grapes and the lime.
4. Stir juice well then divide ice between two tumblers. Pour juice evenly over ice and top glasses up with mineral water or lemonade.
5. Stir and serve immediately.

This recipe makes approximately 300ml (10 fl oz) concentrated juice.

Melon Solo

Serves 2

Melon is a great reviver that's particularly low in calories. Mixing two different kinds of melon gives a wonderful drink. In fact, there's simply nothing quite like it! Melons are natural diuretics and aid in ridding the body of toxins.

Maximum kcals per serving: 32

225g (8oz) slice honeydew melon, with seeds and skin
225g (8oz) slice cantaloupe melon, with seeds and skin

1. Cut the melon slices into pieces that will fit the juicer and store in a bowl.
2. With the motor running, extract juice from the melons. Stir well.
3. Pour into two glasses and serve immediately.

This recipe makes approximately 350ml (12 fl oz) concentrated juice.

Apple and Pear Juice
Serves 2

Different varieties of apples with pears makes a refreshing juice that's full of health. It is important to drink apple juice as soon as it has been made as it discolours quickly when exposed to the air.

Maximum kcals per serving: 89

1 Bramley apple
1 Cox's Orange Pippin apple
1 Spartan apple
1 ripe Williams pear

1. Cut the apples and pear into slices to fit the juicer. Store in a mixing bowl.
2. With the motor running, juice the apples with the pear. Stir juice well.
3. Divide between two tumblers and serve immediately.

This recipe makes approximately 175ml (6 fl oz) concentrated juice.

Fruit Juices

Strawberry and Apple Juice
Serves 2

This refreshing juice is bursting with vitamin C. Serve as an excellent refresher after sport. The ginger adds a mellow richness.

Maximum kcals per serving: 83

10 medium size strawberries
3 Cox's apples
1.25cm (½ inch) piece root ginger (optional)

1. Put strawberries into a bowl beside the juicer.
2. Slice apples to fit the juicer and add to the bowl with the root ginger.
3. With the motor running, juice the strawberries with the apple and root ginger. Stir juice well.
4. Divide between two tumblers and serve immediately.

This recipe makes approximately 350ml (12 fl oz) concentrated juice.

Mango and Tangerine Juice
Serves 3

The flavours of mangoes and tangerines combine well to make a thick juice that tastes terrific diluted with ice cold mineral water on a hot summer's day. Rich in vitamins A and C, this is a very healthy juice.

Maximum kcals per serving: **74**

1 large ripe mango
4 tangerines

To serve
ice cold sparkling mineral water

1. Peel and slice the mango to fit the juicer, discarding the large central stone. Store flesh in a bowl beside the juicer.
2. Peel the tangerines, leaving on most of the white pith. Divide into segments to fit the juicer and add to the bowl.
3. With the motor running, juice the mango flesh and the tangerine. Stir juice well and divide between two tumblers.
4. Top up with ice cold mineral water and stir again before serving, or serve neat.

This recipe makes approximately 250ml (8 fl oz) concentrated juice.

Nectarine, Kiwi and Cherry Juice

Serves 2

Deliciously sweet and fruity yet not too high in calories, this is a wonderful cocktail to serve before dinner instead of gin and tonic!

Maximum kcals per serving: 75

2 nectarines
2 kiwi fruit
6 cherries, Black Heart if possible
1 small wedge lemon
5cm (2 inch) piece cucumber

1. Slice the nectarines to fit the juicer, discarding central stone. Store in a bowl.
2. Slice the unpeeled kiwi fruit and add to the bowl.
3. Remove stones from cherries either by cutting cherries in half and removing stone or by using a cherry pitter.
4. Add cherries to bowl with the lemon and cucumber.
5. Juice the fruits and cucumber. Stir juice well.
6. Divide juice between two tumblers and serve immediately.

This recipe makes approximately 350ml (12 fl oz) concentrated juice.

Strawberry Cooler
Serves 1

An interesting blend of flavours in a pretty, refreshing drink. It is an excellent alternative to a sugary snack and satisfies that craving for something sweet.

Maximum kcals per serving: 120

100g (4oz) medium size strawberries
1 large orange
1 large eating apple

1. Place strawberries in a bowl beside the juicer.
2. Peel orange, slice to fit juicer, discarding pips. Add to bowl.
3. Slice apple to fit juicer. Add to bowl.
4. With the motor running, juice the prepared fruits.
5. Pour into a tumbler and drink immediately.

This recipe makes approximately 250ml (8 fl oz) concentrated juice.

Plum, Raspberry and Grape Juice

Serves 2

Raspberries have a wonderful fresh tangy taste and are a good source of vitamin C. They are low in calories so balance the grapes well in this recipe which is excellent topped up with soda water or diet lemonade.

Maximum kcals per serving: 70

150g (5oz) seedless black grapes
100g (4oz) raspberries
2 ripe plums

To serve
ice cubes
low-calorie lemonade or soda water

1. Discard any old, brown stems from the grapes, divide into small bunches and put them into a bowl, near the juicer. Add the raspberries to the bowl.
2. Halve plums and discard central stone, then slice plums to fit juicer. Add to the bowl.
3. With the motor running, extract juice from the fruit. Stir well.
4. Put ice into two tumblers. Divide juice between the tumblers, pouring it over the ice.
5. Top up each tumbler of fruit juice with lemonade or soda water and stir well. Serve immediately.

This recipe makes approximately 300ml (10 fl oz) concentrated juice.

Sharon Fruit and Melon Juice
Serves 2

Sharon fruit adds a slight taste of mango and spice to this refreshing juice with plenty of vitamins and a lovely sweet taste.

Maximum kcals per serving: 72

1 sharon fruit
8 medium size strawberries
225g (8oz) slice melon, with skin and seeds

To serve
ice cubes

1. Slice the sharon fruit to fit the juicer and store in a mixing bowl.
2. Add strawberries to the mixing bowl.
3. Cut melon into pieces that will fit the juicer and add to the bowl.
4. With the motor running, juice the sharon fruit with the strawberries and melon.
5. Stir the juice and put into two tumblers with ice. Serve immediately.

This recipe makes approximately 350ml (12 fl oz) concentrated juice.

Peach and Cox's Juice
Serves 2

Juicy peaches are so good for you and when combined with apple and cucumber they provide a refreshing, cooling juice. A wonderful reviver after sport.

Maximum kcals per serving: 90

2 ripe peaches
2 Cox's apples
5cm (2 inch) piece cucumber

To serve
ice cubes

1. Cut the peaches into slices to fit the juicer, discarding central stone, and store in a mixing bowl.
2. Cut the apples into slices to fit the juicer and add to the bowl with the cucumber.
3. With the motor running, juice the peaches with the apple and cucumber. Stir juice well.
4. Divide ice cubes between two tumblers. Top up with juice and serve immediately.

This recipe makes approximately 450ml (15 fl oz) concentrated juice.

Pineapple and Satsuma Juice

Serves 2

This is one of my favourite juices. I like it topped up with sparkling mineral water to make a long, thirst-quenching drink that's full of nutrients and flavour.

Maximum kcals per serving: 74

175g (6oz) slice pineapple
2 satsumas
1 Discovery apple or other sweet eating apple

To serve
crushed ice
sparkling mineral water (optional)

1. Cut the pineapple into strips to fit the juicer. Store in a mixing bowl.
2. Peel satsumas and add to mixing bowl.
3. Slice the apple to fit the juicer and add to the bowl.
4. With the motor running, juice the pineapple with the satsumas and the apple.
5. Divide ice between two tumblers. Pour juice over ice. Top up with mineral water, if using, and serve immediately.

This recipe makes approximately 300ml (10 fl oz) concentrated juice.

Fruity Cocktail
Serves 2

Try serving this juice at Christmas-time as a cocktail. It can be topped up with mineral water and served with ice and a slice, or serve it neat. A dieter's treat!

Maximum kcals per serving: 99

225g (8oz) pineapple
1 satsuma
1 ripe Williams pear
100g (4oz) seedless white grapes

1. Cut the pineapple to fit juicer and put in a mixing bowl.
2. Peel the satsuma and add to mixing bowl.
3. Slice pear to juicing size. Add to mixing bowl with the grapes.
4. With motor running, juice the pineapple with the satsuma, pear and grapes.
5. Stir juice well and pour into two tumblers. Serve immediately.

This recipe makes approximately 300ml (10 fl oz) concentrated juice.

Peach, Bramley and Grape Juice
Serves 2

Bramley apples are bursting with vitamin C and flavour. This juice is refreshing and low in calories.

Maximum kcals per serving: 83

2 large ripe peaches
1 Bramley apple, about 225g (8oz)
100g (4oz) seedless grapes

To serve
mineral water

1. Slice the peaches to fit the juicer, discarding the central stone. Store in a mixing bowl.
2. Slice the apple to fit the juicer and add to the bowl.
3. Discard any old, brown stems from the grapes, divide into small bunches and add to the bowl.
4. With the motor running, juice the peaches with the apple and grapes. Stir the juice well.
5. Divide juice between two tumblers. Top up with mineral water and serve immediately.

This recipe makes approximately 350ml (12 fl oz) concentrated juice.

Tangerine, Pineapple and Melon Juice

Serves 2

This fruity cocktail is one of the best pick-me-ups I've ever tried. Fantastically fruity!

Maximum kcals per serving: 75

3 tangerines
175g (6oz) slice pineapple
225g (8oz) slice melon, with skin and seeds
2 sprigs mint

To serve
ice cubes

1. Peel the tangerines. Divide into segments to fit the juicer and store in a mixing bowl.
2. Cut pineapple into strips to fit juicer and add to the bowl.
3. Cut melon into pieces that will fit the juicer and add to the bowl with the mint.
4. With the motor running, juice the tangerines with the pineapple, melon and mint. Stir juice well.
5. Put ice cubes into each of two tumblers. Pour juice over ice and serve immediately.

This recipe makes approximately 400ml (14 fl oz) concentrated juice.

Melon, Orange and Grapefruit Trio

Serves 3

A refreshing trio of fruits, the melon balances the acidity in the citrus fruits. Bursting with vitamin C and full of nutrients.

Maximum kcals per serving: **79**

225g (8oz) slice melon, with skin and seeds
1 orange
1 pink grapefruit

1. Cut melon into slices to fit the juicer. Place in mixing bowl.
2. Peel orange and discard pips. Segment to fit juicer and add to bowl.
3. Peel grapefruit and slice to fit juicer, discarding pips. Add to bowl.
4. With motor running, juice melon with orange and grapefruit.
5. Stir juice well. Serve immediately in three wine glasses.

This recipe makes approximately 475ml (16 fl oz) concentrated juice.

Healthy Breakfast Shake
Serves 2

A healthy alternative to breakfast, this is a nutritious meal in a glass. Quick and easy to prepare, this drink will appeal to teenagers.

Maximum kcals per serving: 100

2 ripe peaches or pears
100g (4oz) seedless black grapes
300ml (10 fl oz) ice cold skimmed milk

1. Slice peaches or pears to fit juicer and store in a mixing bowl. If using peaches, discard central stone.
2. Add grapes to the mixing bowl, discarding any old, brown stems.
3. With motor running, juice the peaches or pears and the grapes.
4. Stir the juice into the milk.
5. Pour the shake into two tumblers and serve immediately.

This recipe makes approximately 650ml (22 fl oz) milk shake.

Special Breakfast Juice
Serves 2

Pineapple is a wonderful source of vitamins and minerals; it helps with digestion, too, and this healthy juice, sipped first thing in the morning, is guaranteed to transport you to that tropical island, even if only momentarily.

Maximum kcals per serving: 85

2.5cm (1 inch) thick slice pineapple, with skin left on
1 large orange
1 pink grapefruit

To serve
ice cubes
sprigs of mint

1. Cut the pineapple round into strips. Store in a mixing bowl.
2. Peel the orange and grapefruit, leaving on about half the pith. Slice the orange and grapefruit into juiceable pieces, discarding pips.
3. With the motor running, extract juice from the fruit. Stir juice well.
4. Put ice cubes into two wine glasses.
5. Pour juice on to ice. Serve immediately, decorating each glass with a sprig of mint.

This recipe makes approximately 300ml (10 fl oz) concentrated juice.

Hurry Breakfast Shake
Serves 1

Specially originated for busy mums who don't have time to prepare breakfast for themselves, this is a delicious breakfast in a glass with plenty of calcium, vitamins and protein. An ideal slimmer's breakfast.

Maximum kcals per serving: 170

175g (6oz) slice melon
4 medium size strawberries
300ml (10 fl oz) ice cold skimmed milk

1. Cut melon to fit juicer and put in a mixing bowl.
2. Add strawberries to mixing bowl.
3. With motor running, juice the melon and strawberries.
4. Blend the juice into the milk.
5. Pour the shake into a tumbler. Serve immediately.

This recipe makes approximately 475ml (16 fl oz) milk shake.

Vegetable Juices

Celery and Beetroot Juice
Serves 1

Healthy raw beetroot is rich in iron and calcium, so enjoy this delicious drink often.

Maximum kcals per serving: **90**

1 orange
2 sticks celery
½ small beetroot
½ handful parsley

To serve
ice cubes

1. Peel orange then slice to fit juicer, discarding pips. Put into a mixing bowl.
2. Cut celery to fit juicer and add to bowl with the beetroot and parsley.
3. With the motor running, juice the orange with the celery, beetroot and parsley. Stir juice well.
4. Put ice cubes into a tumbler. Pour juice over ice and serve immediately.

This recipe makes approximately 300ml (10 fl oz) concentrated juice.

Reviving Juice
Serves 1

An excellent juice to take when you're feeling tired – a good pick you up.

Maximum kcals per serving: 84

2 carrots
1 parsnip
6 sprigs watercress
6 lettuce leaves

1. Cut carrots and parsnip to fit juicer and put into a mixing bowl. Add watercress to the bowl.
2. Tear lettuce to fit juicer and add to the bowl.
3. With the motor running, juice the carrots, parsnip, watercress and lettuce. Stir juice well.
4. Pour into a tumbler and serve immediately.

This recipe makes approximately 300ml (10 fl oz) concentrated juice.

Tomato Solo

Serves 1

Use juicy, ripe, red tomatoes on their own for the most incredible thick juice that's bursting with flavour, vitamins and minerals.

Maximum kcals per serving: 68

4 large ripe tomatoes
6 basil leaves

1. Slice tomatoes to fit the juicer and put into a mixing bowl with the basil leaves.
2. With the motor running, juice the tomatoes with the basil. Stir juice well and pour into a tumbler. Serve immediately.

This recipe makes approximately 250ml (8 fl oz) concentrated juice.

Oriental Juice
Serves 1

Plums and garlic give a delicious flavour to this Chinese-flavoured juice which is packed with vitamins and minerals.

Maximum kcals per serving: 87

2 plums
5cm (2 inch) piece cucumber
75g (3oz) bean shoots
1 clove garlic
2 spring onions
3 sprigs coriander
2 medium size tomatoes

1. Slice plums to fit juicer, discarding central stone. Put into a mixing bowl.
2. Slice cucumber to fit juicer and add to bowl with the bean shoots, garlic, spring onions and coriander.
3. Slice tomatoes to fit juicer and add to bowl.
4. With the motor running, juice the plums with the cucumber, bean shoots, garlic, spring onions, coriander and tomatoes. Stir juice well.
5. Pour into a tumbler and serve immediately.

This recipe makes approximately 300ml (10 fl oz) concentrated juice.

Pineapple Salad Juice
Serves 1

Just as pineapple tastes delicious with leaf salads, it also enhances this salad juice. A healthy tonic in a glass, this long drink has very few calories.

Maximum kcals per serving: 74

2.5cm (1 inch) slice pineapple
1 Little Gem lettuce
1 courgette
1 tomato
15ml (1 tablespoon) chives, freshly chopped
6 basil leaves

1. Cut the pineapple into slices that will fit the juicer. Store in a mixing bowl.
2. Cut the Little Gem lettuce into wedges that will fit the juicer. Add to the bowl.
3. Slice courgette and tomato to fit juicer and add to the bowl with the chives and basil.
4. With the motor running, juice the pineapple with the lettuce, courgette, tomato, chives and basil. Stir juice well.
5. Pour into a tumbler and serve immediately.

This recipe makes approximately 375ml (13 fl oz) concentrated juice.

Carrot, Celery and Apple Juice
Serves 2

A dramatic combination of flavours that's got plenty of zip – a wonderful reviver in the winter and a great source of vitamin A.

Maximum kcals per serving: 70

2 medium size carrots
1 large stick celery
½ apple
2 or 3 coriander leaves

1. If necessary, cut carrots and celery to fit juicer. Cut the apple into slices to fit juicer. Store in a mixing bowl.
2. With the motor running, juice the carrots with the celery, apple and coriander.
3. Stir juice well, divide between two wine glasses and serve immediately.

This recipe makes approximately 275ml (9 fl oz) concentrated juice.

Vegetable Juices

Carrot, Pear and Broccoli Juice
Serves 1

Sweet ripe pears give a wonderful mellow flavour to this delicious juice with plenty of vitamins A and C. Nice and filling, too.

Maximum kcals per serving: 86

1 ripe Williams pear
2 medium size carrots
3 broccoli florets, with stems

1. Slice the pear to fit the juicer and store in a mixing bowl.
2. Slice the carrots to fit the juicer and add to the bowl with the broccoli.
3. With the motor running, juice the pear with the carrots and broccoli.
4. Stir the juice, pour into a tumbler and serve immediately.

This recipe makes approximately 250ml (8 fl oz) concentrated juice.

Broccoli, Sprout and Apple Juice
Serves 1

This is a real health juice that's bursting with vitamins and minerals so serve it regularly. You'll be surprised how delicious it tastes.

Maximum kcals per serving: **111**

3 broccoli florets, with stems
4 Brussels sprouts
1½ eating apples

1. Put the broccoli and sprouts into a mixing bowl.
2. Slice the apples to fit the juicer and add to the bowl.
3. With the motor running, juice the broccoli with the sprouts and apple.
4. Stir juice well. Pour into a tumbler and serve immediately.

This recipe makes approximately 175ml (6 fl oz) concentrated juice.

Vegetable Juices

Carrot, Pineapple and Cucumber Juice

Serves 1

Pineapple gives a wonderful flavour to this thick frothy juice that can be diluted with mineral water and is high on nutrients.

Maximum kcals per serving: 71

2 medium size carrots
75g (3oz) slice fresh pineapple
2.5cm (1 inch) slice cucumber

1. Slice the carrots to fit the juicer and store in a mixing bowl.
2. Slice the pineapple to fit the juicer and add to the bowl with the cucumber.
3. With the motor running, juice the carrots with the pineapple and cucumber. Stir juice well.
4. Pour into a tumbler and serve immediately.

This recipe makes approximately 300ml (10 fl oz) concentrated juice.

Carrot, Sharon Fruit and Parsley Juice
Serves 1

Carrot and sharon fruit taste wonderful together and make a delicious drink that's excellent diluted with mineral water. Plenty of vitamins A and C.

Maximum kcals per serving: 99

3 medium size carrots
1 sharon fruit
4 sprigs parsley

To serve
mineral water (optional)

1. Cut the carrots into pieces to fit juicer. Put into a mixing bowl.
2. Slice sharon fruit to fit juicer. Add to mixing bowl.
3. Put parsley sprigs into the mixing bowl.
4. With the motor running, juice the carrots with the sharon fruit and parsley.
5. Stir juice well, then serve with mineral water, if required.

This recipe makes approximately 250ml (8 fl oz) concentrated juice.

Spinach, Tomato and Celery Juice

Serves 1

A refreshing mix of vegetables that tastes extremely palatable. A good supply of vitamin C.

Maximum kcals per serving: 67

4 tomatoes
2 celery stalks
6 spinach leaves
Few sprigs celery leaves

1. Slice tomatoes to fit juicer and store in a mixing bowl.
2. Cut celery to fit juicer and add to bowl.
3. Roll up each spinach leaf fairly tightly and add to the bowl with the celery leaves.
4. With the motor running, juice the tomatoes with the celery, rolled spinach leaves and the celery leaves. Stir juice well.
5. Pour into a tumbler and serve immediately.

This recipe makes approximately 250ml (8 fl oz) concentrated juice.

Carrot, Cauliflower, Orange and Parsnip Juice

Serves 1 or 2

A well-flavoured juice to help take away those hunger pangs, and a low-calorie reviver.

Maximum kcals per serving: 55

2 medium size carrots
3 cauliflower florets
1 medium orange
75g (3oz) parsnips

1. Cut carrots to fit juicer and store in a mixing bowl.
2. Add cauliflower florets to the bowl.
3. Peel and slice orange to fit juicer, discarding pips. Add to bowl.
4. Slice parsnips to fit juicer. Add to bowl.
5. With the motor running, juice the carrots with the cauliflower, orange and parsnips. Stir juice well.
6. Pour into a tumbler and serve immediately.

This recipe makes approximately 350ml (12 fl oz) concentrated juice.

Green Pepper, Carrot and Sharon Fruit Juice

Serves 1

Plenty of vitamin A and C in this tasty thick juice. Serve topped up with mineral water, if preferred, for a long cool drink.

Maximum kcals per serving: **100**

¼ medium green pepper
1 sharon fruit
2 medium size carrots
5cm (2 inch) slice cucumber

To serve
chilled mineral water, if required

1. Slice green pepper to fit juicer if necessary and put into a mixing bowl.
2. Slice sharon fruit to fit juicer and add to the bowl.
3. Slice carrots to fit juicer and add to bowl with the cucumber.
4. With the motor running, juice the green pepper with the sharon fruit, carrots and cucumber.
5. Stir juice well, pour into a tumbler and serve immediately, topping the juice up with mineral water if required.

This recipe makes approximately 175ml (6 fl oz) concentrated juice.

Vegetable Medley with Apple Juice

Serves 1

Excellent for colds or just as a boost when you're feeling tired – a true tonic!

Maximum kcals per serving: 97

3 medium size carrots
1 apple
1 large stick celery
2 medium tomatoes
½ handful parsley sprigs

1. Cut carrots into pieces to fit juicer and store in a mixing bowl.
2. Slice apple to fit juicer and add to the bowl.
3. Cut celery stick in half and add to bowl.
4. Cut tomatoes into juiceable pieces and add to the bowl with the parsley sprigs.
5. With the motor running, juice the carrots, apple, celery, tomatoes and parsley. Stir juice well.
6. Pour into a tumbler and serve immediately.

This recipe makes approximately 300ml (10 fl oz) concentrated juice.

Vegetable Juices 61

Ginger, Carrot and Apple Juice with Tomato

Serves 1 or 2

Try to use Cox's Orange Pippins for this juice, if possible. The ginger adds a subtle warmth to the drink.

Maximum kcals per serving: 109

2.5cm (1 inch) piece root ginger (optional)
1 eating apple, Cox's if possible
2 medium size tomatoes
2 medium size carrots

1. Peel the ginger if skin is very thick then put into a mixing bowl.
2. Slice apple to fit juicer and add to bowl.
3. Slice tomatoes to fit juicer. Cut carrots to fit juicer. Add both to the bowl.
4. With the motor running, juice the ginger with the apple, tomatoes and carrots.
5. Stir juice well, pour into a tumbler and serve immediately.

This recipe makes approximately 325ml (11 fl oz) concentrated juice.

Tomato and Celery Juice

Serves 1

Celery tastes super healthy when juiced with tomatoes. A real refresher and a good reviver after sport.

Maximum kcals per serving: 65

2 large sticks celery
3 large ripe tomatoes
4 sprigs parsley

1. Cut celery into pieces to fit juicer and store in a mixing bowl.
2. Slice tomatoes to fit juicer and add to the bowl.
3. Add parsley to the bowl.
4. With the motor running, juice the celery and tomatoes with the parsley.
5. Stir juice well, pour into a tumbler and serve immediately.

This recipe makes approximately 250ml (8 fl oz) concentrated juice.

Spring Vegetable Tonic
Serves 1

Pineapple tastes wonderful with cucumber, parsley and celery. Use this juice as a terrific spring cleaner for bodies! Great instead of a cup of tea in the afternoon.

Maximum kcals per serving: 117

5cm (2 inch) slice fresh pineapple
5cm (2 inch) piece cucumber
1 celery stalk
½ handful parsley sprigs

To serve
crushed ice
sparkling mineral water

1. Cut the pineapple into strips to fit the juicer. Store in a mixing bowl.
2. Cut cucumber and celery to fit juicer and add to the bowl with the parsley.
3. With the motor running, juice the pineapple with the cucumber, celery and parsley. Stir juice well.
4. Put some crushed ice into a tall tumbler. Top up with juice and add mineral water. Serve immediately.

This recipe makes approximately 150ml (5 fl oz) concentrated juice.

Cabbage Cocktail

Serves 1 or 2

A delicious juice with a bit of a kick provided by the radishes. A great veggie drink.

Maximum kcals per serving: 100

100g (4oz) Savoy cabbage
100g (4oz) seedless green grapes
2 carrots
3 radishes
½ handful parsley

To serve
ice cubes
mineral water (optional)

1. Cut the cabbage into wedges that will fit the juicer. Store in a mixing bowl.
2. Cut the grapes into bunches that will fit the juicer and add to the bowl, discarding any old, brown stems.
3. Cut carrots to fit the juicer and add to the bowl with the radishes and parsley.
4. With the motor running, juice the cabbage with the grapes, carrots, radishes and parsley. Stir juice well.
5. Put ice into a tumbler. Top up with juice, add mineral water and serve immediately.

This recipe makes approximately 175ml (6 fl oz) concentrated juice.

Cabbage, Tomato and Apple Juice

Serves 1

Plenty of vitamins and minerals in this juice which will act as a natural diuretic.

Maximum kcals per serving: 100

1 parsnip
50g (2oz) green cabbage
1 eating apple
1 medium size tomato

To serve
ice cubes

1. Cut parsnip in half and put into a mixing bowl beside the juicer.
2. Cut cabbage to fit juicer and add to the bowl.
3. Slice apple and tomato to fit juicer and add to bowl.
4. With the motor running, juice the parsnip with the cabbage, apple and tomato. Stir juice well.
5. Put ice into a tumbler. Top up with juice and serve immediately.

This recipe makes approximately 250ml (8 fl oz) concentrated juice.

Carrot, Garlic and Celery Juice
Serves 2

Garlic has been used for centuries for its healing properties. Drinking garlic in juice is an excellent way of taking it naturally. Juice a few more vegetables after you've juiced garlic to free the machine of this rather pungent little bulb.

Maximum kcals per serving: 92

100g (4oz) cabbage
3 medium size carrots
½ clove garlic
1 large stick celery, with leaves
5cm (2 inch) slice cucumber

1. Cut cabbage and carrots to fit juicer and store in a mixing bowl. Add garlic to the bowl.
2. Cut celery to fit juicer and add to the bowl with the cucumber.
3. With the motor running, juice the cabbage with the carrots, garlic, celery and cucumber. Stir juice well.
4. Pour into a tumbler and serve immediately.

This recipe makes approximately 275ml (9 fl oz) concentrated juice.

Carrot and Tomato Juice

Serves 1

Carrot and tomato combine well to produce a thick juice that's bursting with vitamins. Drink this one regularly, diluted with mineral water if required.

Maximum kcals per serving: 65

3 medium size carrots
2 medium size ripe tomatoes
6 sprigs parsley

To serve
mineral water (optional)

1. Cut carrots to fit juicer and store in a mixing bowl.
2. Slice tomatoes to fit juicer and add to the bowl.
3. Put parsley into the bowl.
4. With the motor running, juice the carrots with the tomatoes and parsley. Stir juice well.
5. Pour into a tumbler and serve immediately, topped up with mineral water if required.

This recipe makes approximately 200ml (7 fl oz) concentrated juice.

Tomato, Cucumber and Pepper Juice

Serves 1

A tangy salad juice that's bursting with vitamins and minerals.

Maximum kcals per serving: 72

2 tomatoes
2.5cm (1 inch) slice cucumber
100g (4oz) seedless grapes
½ green pepper
25g (1oz) watercress

1. Slice tomatoes and cucumber to fit the juicer and store in a mixing bowl.
2. Cut grapes into bunches to fit juicer, discarding any old, brown stems, and add to the bowl with the pepper and watercress.
3. With the motor running, juice the tomatoes with the cucumber, grapes, pepper and watercress. Stir juice well.
4. Pour juice into a tumbler and serve immediately.

This recipe makes approximately 275ml (9 fl oz) concentrated juice.

Spinach, Carrot and Fennel Juice
Serves 1

A refreshing juice that's good after sport. Serve with mineral water if required.

Maximum kcals per serving: 44

6 spinach leaves
1 medium carrot
½ medium fennel
1 celery stalk

To serve
ice cubes
mineral water (optional)

1. Roll the spinach leaves and put into a mixing bowl.
2. Cut the carrot and fennel into pieces to fit the juicer and add to the bowl with the celery.
3. With the motor running, juice the spinach with the carrot, fennel and celery. Stir juice well.
4. Put ice cubes into a tumbler. Pour juice over ice cubes, top up with mineral water if using and serve immediately.

This recipe makes approximately 250ml (8 fl oz) concentrated juice.

Salad Juice 1
Serves 1

A refreshing juice to serve on a hot summer's day. The lime adds a tang to this salad in a glass.

Maximum kcals per serving: 57

2 large ripe tomatoes
1 small celery stalk
5cm (2 inch) piece cucumber
4 lettuce leaves
1 small wedge lime, peeled

1. Slice tomatoes and put into a medium size mixing bowl.
2. Add celery to the bowl.
3. Cut cucumber to fit juicer if necessary and add to bowl.
4. Roll lettuce leaves and add to bowl. Add lime.
5. With the motor running, juice the tomatoes with the celery, cucumber, lettuce and lime.
6. Stir the juice well and pour into a tumbler. Serve immediately.

This recipe makes approximately 300ml (10 fl oz) concentrated juice.

Salad Juice 2
Serves 1

Mint and coriander give this salad juice a delicious light flavour. A tasty drink for slimmers.

Maximum kcals per serving: 92

50g (2oz) French green beans
1 spring onion
2 courgettes
2 carrots
1 small new potato
8 coriander leaves
2 sprigs young mint

1. Put the beans into a mixing bowl. Add the spring onion.
2. Slice the courgettes and carrots to fit the juicer and add to the bowl.
3. Add the potato to the bowl with the coriander and mint.
4. With the motor running, juice the green beans with the spring onion, courgettes, carrots, potato, coriander and mint. Stir juice well.
5. Pour into a tumbler and serve immediately.

This recipe makes approximately 275ml (9 fl oz) concentrated juice.

Carrot, Mangetout and Broccoli Juice

Serves 1 or 2

This calming juice soothes frazzled nerves and acts as a reviving tonic. Serve with mineral water.

Maximum kcals per serving: 60

½ eating apple
4 carrots
6 mangetout
3 broccoli florets
2.5cm (1 inch) piece cucumber
½ handful parsley sprigs

To serve
ice cold mineral water

1. Slice apple and cut carrots to fit juicer and store in a mixing bowl. Add mangetout, broccoli, cucumber and parsley to the bowl.
2. With the motor running, juice the apple with the carrots, mangetout, broccoli, cucumber and parsley. Stir juice well.
3. Pour juice into a tumbler and top up with mineral water. Stir and serve.

This recipe makes approximately 300ml (10 fl oz) concentrated juice.

Tomato, Melon and Cucumber Juice
Serves 1

This excellent trio tastes fresh and fruity, and is a good natural diuretic.

Maximum kcals per serving: 54

5cm (2 inch) piece cucumber
150g (5oz) slice melon, with skin and seeds
2 medium size ripe tomatoes

1. Slice cucumber to fit juicer and store in a mixing bowl.
2. Slice melon to fit juicer and add to the bowl.
3. Slice tomatoes to fit juicer and add to the bowl.
4. With the motor running, juice the cucumber with the melon and tomatoes. Stir juice well.
5. Pour into tumbler and serve immediately.

This recipe makes approximately 250ml (8 fl oz) concentrated juice.

Snacks, Starters, Soups and Dressings

Homemade Fruity Muesli
Serves 4

Proper muesli is made in advance, giving the oats time to soak in the fruit juice, but you can make this muesli and use immediately, the only difference being that it won't soak up all the fruit juice. This recipe is just like the muesli I tasted in Switzerland – fruity, delicious and certainly filling.

Preparation time: 10 mins + soaking time
Cooking time: 0
Kcals per serving: 204 with yoghurt, 217 with milk

Start to prepare the muesli at least 4 hours in advance or the night before.

For the juicer
1 medium orange
½ pink grapefruit
1 kiwi fruit

75g (3oz) porridge oats
50g (2oz) sultanas
2 apples
1 large banana
60ml (4 tablespoons) low-fat plain yoghurt **or** 140ml (12 fl oz) skimmed milk

1. Either 4 hours in advance or the night before, peel and segment the orange and grapefruit. Store in a mixing bowl.
2. Slice kiwi fruit to fit juicer and add to the bowl.

3. With the motor running, juice the orange, grapefruit and kiwi fruit.
4. Put the oats into a large mixing bowl with the sultanas. Pour over the juice from the juicer. Stir to mix, then cover with cling film and set aside for 4 hours or overnight.
5. When ready to serve, divide muesli between four serving bowls.
6. Core and chop apples and divide between bowls. Peel and slice banana and divide between bowls.
7. Top each serving with 15ml (1 tablespoon) yoghurt or pour 85ml (3 fl oz) milk over each serving.
8. Serve immediately.

Snacks, Starters, Soups and Dressings 79

Fruity Snack
Serves 4

A mixture of dried and fresh fruits in a tangy fruity dressing served with low-fat fromage frais makes an interesting filling snack that's bursting with flavour and high on fibre, vitamins and minerals.

Preparation time: 10 mins
Cooking time: 0
Kcals per serving: 115

For the juicer
1 medium orange, peeled and cut to fit juicer
100g (4oz) seedless grapes, prepared to fit juicer
Grated rind ½ lemon

2 medium size ripe Williams pears, cored and chopped
1 Ogen melon
1 red skinned eating apple, cored and chopped roughly
6 dried apricots, chopped roughly

To serve
60ml (4 tablespoons) low-fat fromage frais
25g (1oz) pistachio nuts, chopped

1. With the motor running, juice the oranges with the grapes. Stir the lemon rind into the juice and pour into a serving dish.
2. Add the pears to the serving dish.
3. Halve the melon and discard the seeds, then either remove the flesh using a melon baller or peel and dice the flesh and add to the serving dish.

4. Add apple and dried apricots to the dish. Toss to coat all fruits with the juice.
5. Serve the fruity snack in four bowls, topping each serving with 15ml (1 tablespoon) fromage frais and a few pistachio nuts.

Mexican Salad

Serves 4

A delicious lunch time snack which doubles as an interesting starter. The juicy dressing adds plenty of tasty moistness with few calories.

Preparation time: 10 mins
Cooking time: 0
Kcals per serving: 160

For the juicer
1 carrot, cut to fit juicer
1 large stick celery, cut to fit juicer
2 medium size tomatoes, cut to fit juicer
1 clove garlic, peeled

225g (8oz) prawns, peeled
1 ripe avocado, peeled and chopped
4 pimento-stuffed olives, sliced
225g (8oz) red pepper, seeded and chopped
4 spring onions, chopped
1 large courgette, diced
Salt and freshly ground black pepper

To serve
mixed salad leaves such as chicory, radicchio, Little Gem lettuce

To garnish
sprigs fresh parsley

1. With the motor running, juice the carrot with the celery, tomatoes and garlic. Set aside.

2. Put the prawns into a large mixing bowl, add the avocado, olives, red pepper, spring onions and courgette.
3. Add a seasoning of salt and pepper to the juice from the juicer. Stir well and pour over salad. Toss to coat.
4. Arrange the salad leaves on four side plates. Top evenly with the prepared Mexican salad and serve immediately, garnished with the parsley.

Ricotta with Apple and Walnuts
Serves 4

Low-fat ricotta cheese makes a tasty low-calorie starter when combined with nectarines and apple juice, herbs, apples and a few chopped walnuts. Serve with water biscuits or Ryvita and a salad garnish for a filling quick meal.

Preparation time: 10 mins
Cooking time: 0
Kcals per serving: 84

For the juicer
1 small nectarine, sliced to fit juicer, discarding central stone
50g (2oz) eating apple, sliced to fit juicer
2 sprigs celery leaves

30ml (2 tablespoons) freshly chopped herbs (parsley, chives, dill, oregano)
225g (8oz) ricotta cheese
Salt and freshly ground black pepper
1 × 100g (4oz) Cox's apple
Few drops lemon juice
25g (1oz) chopped walnuts

To serve
Ryvita biscuits
salad garnish

1. With the motor running, juice the nectarine with the apple and the celery leaves. Stir the herbs into the juice.
2. Turn the ricotta into a mixing bowl. Gradually beat in the juice from the juicer then season to taste with salt and pepper.

Snacks, Starters, Soups and Dressings

3. Peel, core and dice the Cox's apple fairly finely. Toss in the lemon juice.
4. Fold the apple into the cheese mixture.
5. Press the cheese mixture into a small round sundae dish to shape it, then turn out onto a flat surface and serve, cut into 4 wedges sprinkled with chopped walnuts.

Cottage Cheese Pockets
Serves 4

Wholemeal pitta bread briefly warmed under the grill then filled with salad tossed in a lime dressing and topped with cottage cheese and chives, makes an interesting and filling snack meal that's fast to put together.

Preparation time: 10 mins
Cooking time: 5 mins
Kcals per serving: 269

For the juicer
½ lime, peeled and cut to fit juicer, discarding pips
100g (4oz) seedless grapes, prepared to fit juicer
½ handful mixed herbs (parsley, basil, coriander, chives)

3 tomatoes, chopped
½ large cucumber, diced
1 green pepper, seeded and chopped
4 spring onions, chopped
Salt and freshly ground black pepper
4 wholemeal pitta breads
8 black olives, stoned
225g (8oz) cottage cheese with chives
25g (1oz) chopped walnuts

1. With the motor running, juice the lime with the grapes and herbs. Set aside.
2. Put the tomatoes into a mixing bowl. Add the cucumber, pepper and spring onions. Season with a little salt and pepper.

3. Stir the juice then pour it over the salad in the large bowl. Toss to coat.
4. Warm the pitta breads under a hot grill then split them open. Fill with salad, adding 2 olives to each pitta.
5. Top the salad pittas evenly with the cottage cheese and sprinkle with walnuts before serving.

Snacks, Starters, Soups and Dressings

Smoked Trout Salad
Serves 4

A tasty salad that can be put together at the last minute. Serve as a starter or a light lunch.

Preparation time: 10 mins
Cooking time: 0
Kcals per serving: 125

For the juicer
½ medium size carrot, cut to fit juicer
½ Cox's apple, sliced to fit juicer

2 Little Gem lettuces
½ cucumber, diced
2 sticks celery, chopped
2 spring onions, chopped
85ml (3 fl oz) Greek yoghurt (6% fat variety)
30ml (2 tablespoons) freshly chopped oregano
Salt and freshly ground black pepper
4 black olives, stoned
4 × 65g (2½oz) portions smoked trout, skinned
2 × 100g (4oz) eating apples, Cox's if possible, cored and diced

1. With the motor running, juice the carrot with the apple. Set aside.
2. Tear the lettuce into small pieces and put into a large bowl with the cucumber, celery and spring onions. Toss together briefly.
3. Put the yoghurt into a mixing bowl. Stir in the prepared juice with the oregano and a seasoning of salt and pepper.

4. Arrange salad on four side plates. Add an olive to each plate with a serving of trout. Arrange the diced apple on top.
5. Place a dessertspoon of dressing on each starter and serve immediately.

Melon with Prawns and Strawberry Dressing

Serves 4

Fresh ripe Ogen melon served with plump prawns tossed in a refreshing strawberry dressing, what better way is there to start a special dinner party?

Preparation time: 10 mins
Cooking time: 0
Kcals per serving: 125

For the juice dressing
225g (8oz) fresh strawberries, sliced to fit juicer
3 sprigs fresh mint
1 wedge lime, peeled
1 clove garlic
6 fresh basil leaves
15ml (1 tablespoon) olive oil
Salt and freshly ground black pepper

2 ripe Ogen melons
350g (12oz) peeled cooked prawns
100g (4oz) strawberries, sliced

To serve
30ml (2 tablespoons) sesame seeds, toasted
sprigs of parsley

1. With the motor running, juice the strawberries with the mint, lime, garlic and basil. Whisk in the olive oil and a seasoning of salt and pepper. Set aside.

2. Halve the melons, discard the seeds and scoop out the flesh. Retain the shells.
3. Dice the melon flesh and put it with any juice into a mixing bowl. Add the prawns and the strawberries. Pour over the juice dressing. Toss to coat.
4. Arrange melon shells on four side plates. Fill with fruit and prawn mixture and serve immediately sprinkled with the sesame seeds and garnished with parsley sprigs.

Smoked Salmon and Prawns with Lump Fish Roe and Yoghurt
Serves 4

Smoked salmon soaked in fresh lemon and lime juice tastes out of this world. Serve with a few grinds of black pepper and wholemeal toast or rye bread.

Preparation time: 10 mins
Cooking time: 0
Kcals per serving: 121

For the juicer
½ lemon
1 lime
3 sprigs fresh coriander

225g (8oz) smoked salmon
100g (4oz) large prawns, peeled
75ml (4 rounded tablespoons) Greek yoghurt (6% fat variety)
75g (3oz) jar lump fish roe
Freshly ground black pepper

To serve
sprigs of coriander

1. Remove the zest from the lemon using either a grater or a citrus zester. Set aside.
2. Peel the lime and the lemon removing all pith. Slice to fit juicer, discarding pips.
3. Juice the lemon and lime with the coriander. Remove the head from the juice and discard by scooping it off with a spoon.

Snacks, Starters, Soups and Dressings

4. Arrange slices of salmon on four side plates. Add prawns.
5. Stir the lemon zest into the juice then pour evenly over the salmon. Set aside for 10 minutes for flavours to penetrate.
6. When ready to serve, spoon yoghurt onto each plate. Top with 5ml (1 teaspoon) lump fish roe and serve immediately with a grind of pepper and a sprig of coriander to garnish.

Mixed Seafood Salad
Serves 4

Mixed seafoods with baby button mushrooms in a garlicky dressing quickly made in the juicer provides a speedy lunch or suppertime snack that also works well as a starter for entertaining. Serve with French bread or just with a salad garnish.

Preparation time: 12 mins
Cooking time: 2 mins
Kcals per serving: 180

225g (8oz) raw scallops, cleaned
225g (8oz) large cooked prawns, peeled
225g (8oz) cooked crab meat
100g (4oz) baby button mushrooms, sliced
1 shallot, chopped
1 medium size ripe Italian plum tomato

For the juice dressing
1 lime
1 tomato, sliced to fit juicer
6 sprigs parsley
4 sprigs thyme
1 clove garlic
Salt and freshly ground black pepper
2.5ml (½ teaspoon) demerara sugar
15ml (1 tablespoon) olive oil

To serve
Little Gem lettuce leaves
few radicchio leaves

4 whole prawns in their shells
finely chopped parsley

1. Poach the scallops in simmering water for 1–2 minutes, until tender and cooked. Drain and set aside to cool.
2. Put the prawns into a mixing bowl. Add the crab meat, mushrooms and shallot. Peel and chop the tomato, discarding seeds and add to the bowl with the cooled scallops.
3. Prepare the dressing. Remove rind from the lime with a zester. Retain, then peel the lime and slice to fit juicer, discarding pips.
4. With the motor running, juice the lime and the tomato with the parsley, thyme and garlic. Season the juice with a little salt and pepper. Stir in reserved zest and whisk in the sugar and oil to form an emulsion.
5. Pour dressing over seafood. Toss lightly to coat, then set aside for 10–15 minutes for flavours to mingle.
6. Shred the Little Gem lettuce leaves and the radicchio leaves. Divide between four side plates. Top with the seafood mixture and garnish with the whole prawns. Sprinkle with the freshly chopped parsley before serving.

Eggs with Mushrooms and Tomatoes

Serves 4

A speedy lunch or supper snack menu that's filling and nutritious. The mushrooms and juice convert plain scrambled eggs into a very special treat. As eggs are fairly high in cholesterol, only serve this dish once a week.

Preparation time: 10 mins
Cooking time: 12 mins
Kcals per serving: 204 (including 1 slice toast)

For the juicer
3 ripe tomatoes, cut to fit juicer
½ handful parsley
½ small onion

8 eggs, size 3
Salt and freshly ground black pepper
25g (1oz) low-fat spread
225g (8oz) oyster mushrooms, finely chopped

To serve
wholemeal toast
freshly chopped parsley

1. With the motor running, juice the tomatoes with the parsley and onion.
2. Crack the eggs into a large mixing bowl. Beat well, then beat in the prepared juice and a seasoning of salt and pepper.

3. Heat low-fat spread in a large pan until melted.
4. Pour the egg mixture into the pan with the mushrooms. Heat gently, stirring frequently until mixture just sets, 10–12 minutes.
5. Serve immediately on wholemeal toast and sprinkle with chopped parsley.

Creamy Jackets with Tuna
Serves 4

Jacket potatoes make a wonderfully warming meal but they're death to any diet when filled with butter or grated cheese. Try this low-calorie creamy filling which is tasty yet low in calories, making this a high fibre snack.

Preparation time: 10 mins
Cooking time: 1¼–1½ hours or 18 mins in microwave
Kcals per serving: 178

For the juicer
2 tomatoes, sliced to fit juicer
½ handful fresh basil leaves
1 clove garlic (optional)
2 spring onions

4 × 225g (8oz) baking potatoes
75g (3oz) low-fat fromage frais
30ml (2 tablespoons) reduced calorie mayonnaise
10ml (2 teaspoons) paprika
Salt
1 × 198g (7oz) can tuna fish in brine, drained

To serve
salad garnish (plenty of lettuce, celery, tomatoes, cucumber, beetroot)

1. Pre-heat the oven to 200°C (400°F) gas mark 6. Prick the potatoes, arrange on baking sheet and bake for 1¼–1½ hours, until tender. Alternatively, if you have a microwave, arrange the pricked potatoes in a circle on a

dinner plate. Microwave on 100%/FULL power for 18 minutes. Allow to stand for 7 minutes.
2. Meanwhile, with the motor running, juice the tomatoes with the basil, garlic and onions.
3. Turn the fromage frais into a mixing bowl. Stir in the mayonnaise and paprika. Add the juice from the juicer, stirring until blended. Season with a little salt.
4. Split the potatoes open. Divide the filling between them and serve immediately, topping each one with drained tuna, and accompany with a salad garnish.

Snacks, Starters, Soups and Dressings

Bouillabaisse
Serves 4

Fish soup is a very popular starter in Mediterranean countries. Serve with wholemeal bread (without butter or other spread) to help soak up the delicious liquid.

Note: As the soup comes to the boil, you may prefer to spoon off and discard the scum that appears.

Preparation time: 10 mins
Cooking time: 21 mins
Kcals per serving: 190

For the juicer
½ orange, peeled and cut to fit juicer
1 carrot, cut to fit juicer
225g (8oz) tomatoes, cut to fit juicer
45ml (3 tablespoons) tomato purée

750g (1½lb) mixed fish and shellfish, e.g. cod, whiting, bass, trout, raw prawns, crab, a few mussels
15ml (1 tablespoon) olive oil
2 red skinned onions, sliced thinly
1 celery stick, chopped
2 garlic cloves, crushed
100g (4oz) baby sweetcorn, halved
30ml (2 tablespoons) freshly chopped parsley
Salt and freshly ground black pepper
1 bay leaf
900ml (1½ pints) fish stock

To serve
30ml (2 tablespoons) freshly chopped parsley

chunks of wholemeal or granary bread

1. With the motor running, juice the orange with the carrot and the tomatoes. Blend tomato purée into juice and set aside.
2. Skin and fillet the fish if necessary then cut into chunks. Remove shellfish from their shells, except for the mussels.
3. Heat oil in a large saucepan. Add the onions, celery and garlic and sauté gently for 8–10 minutes, until softened. Add fish, except shellfish, and the sweetcorn to the pan, in a single layer, if possible.
4. Add prepared juice to the pan with the parsley, a seasoning of salt and pepper, the bay leaf and stock. Bring to the boil, cover and simmer for about 6–8 minutes, stirring once or twice until fish is just cooked.
5. Add shellfish and continue to cook, covered, for a further 5 minutes. Discard any mussels that do not open. Remove the bay leaf.
6. Ladle into soup bowls and serve immediately sprinkled with the parsley and accompanied by the bread.

Vegetable Soup

Serves 4

Served as a starter or a light supper or lunch, this warming soup is bursting with flavour and is guaranteed to appeal to all.

Preparation time: 15 mins
Cooking time: 37 mins
Kcals per serving: 118

For the juicer
4 medium size ripe tomatoes, cut to fit juicer
½ handful of fresh oregano

15ml (1 tablespoon) olive oil
1 clove garlic, crushed
1 red onion, peeled and sliced
2 carrots, peeled and sliced
1 green pepper, seeded and chopped
1 courgette, sliced
15ml (1 tablespoon) tomato purée
1.2 litres (2 pints) chicken stock
Freshly ground black pepper
10ml (2 teaspoons) cornflour
50g (2oz) dried soup pasta shapes
75g (3oz) frozen sweetcorn kernels
30ml (2 tablespoons) freshly chopped parsley

1. With the motor running, juice the tomatoes with the oregano. Set juice aside.
2. Heat the oil in a large saucepan. Add the garlic, onion, carrots and pepper and sauté for 2–3 minutes.

3. Add the courgette, tomato purée and stock to the pan with the prepared juice. Season with the black pepper.
4. Bring to the boil, cover and simmer gently for 20–25 minutes until vegetables are just tender.
5. Blend cornflour to a smooth paste with 15ml (1 tablespoon) water. Stir into soup, then stir pasta, sweetcorn and parsley into soup. Return to boil, stirring, then simmer, uncovered, for 6–8 minutes until pasta is cooked.
6. Serve immediately.

Lentil and Tomato Soup
Serves 4

A well-flavoured healthy soup that's nice and creamy. Ideal for vegetarians, serve with wholemeal or granary bread for a high fibre snack.

Preparation time: 10 mins
Cooking time: 20 mins
Kcals per serving: 133

For the juicer
½ handful parsley sprigs
1 medium onion, cut to fit juicer
6 large ripe tomatoes, sliced to fit juicer

10ml (2 teaspoons) olive oil
1 medium carrot, diced
3 small new potatoes, diced
75g (3oz) red split lentils
600ml (1 pint) vegetable stock
Salt and freshly ground black pepper

To garnish
few snipped chives

1. With the motor running, juice the parsley with the onion and tomatoes. Stir juice and set aside.
2. Heat the oil in a large saucepan, then sauté the carrot and potatoes for 5 minutes. Stir in the lentils.
3. Add the juice from the juicer with the stock. Season with a little salt and pepper.

4. Bring to the boil, stirring occasionally. Cover with a lid and simmer for 20 minutes.
5. Using a draining spoon, transfer carrots, lentils and potato to a food processor, add about 150ml (5 fl oz) of the soup liquid and blend until smooth.
6. Return the purée to the soup liquid in the pan.
7. Stir well. Re-heat to serving temperature and serve immediately, garnished with the chives.

Beefy Vegetable Soup
Serves 4

I love carrots with beef stock but chicken or vegetable stock may be used if preferred. A filling soup with plenty of fibre and very little fat.

Preparation time: 10 mins
Cooking time: 25 mins
Kcals per serving: 56

For the juicer
1 large onion, cut to fit juicer
2 medium size tomatoes, cut to fit juicer
1 clove garlic (optional)
1 stick celery
½ handful fresh coriander

450g (1lb) carrots, sliced
175g (6oz) parsnips, diced
600ml (1 pint) beef stock
Salt and freshly ground black pepper
60ml (4 tablespoons) skimmed milk

To serve
freshly chopped coriander

1. With the motor running, juice the onion with the tomatoes, garlic, celery and coriander.
2. Place the carrots and parsnips in a large saucepan. Pour over the juice from the juicer and the stock. Season with a little salt and pepper. Bring to the boil, stirring occasionally.

3. Cover with a lid and simmer for 20–25 minutes, until vegetables are tender.
4. Transfer to food processor and blend to a purée. (Blend in batches if necessary.)
5. Remove blade and return purée to saucepan, add milk. Stir to blend well. Return soup to simmering point, stirring.
6. Serve the soup sprinkled with coriander.

Stir-fries

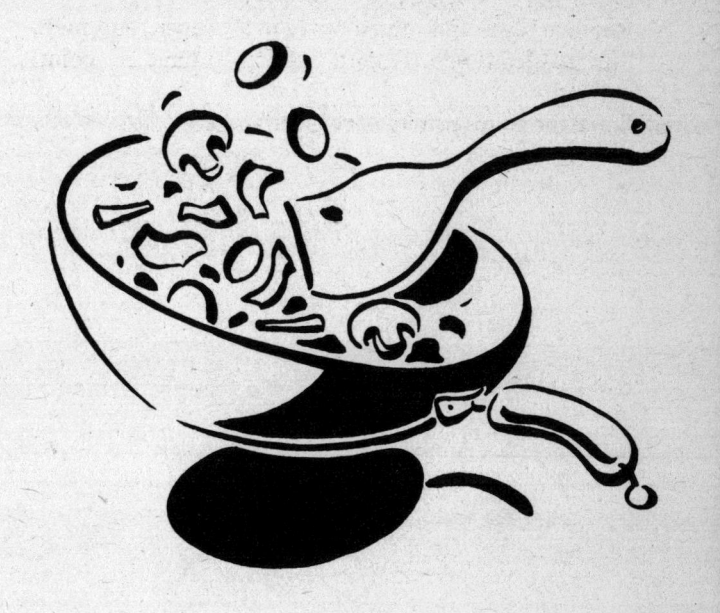

Chicken and Cashew Stir-fry

Serves 4

Low-calorie chicken with crunchy vegetables and a few cashew nuts – you'll forget you're counting calories. Serve with boiled rice or noodles.

Preparation time: 10 mins
Cooking time: 10 mins
Kcals per serving: 259

For the juicer
3 medium size ripe tomatoes, cut to fit juicer
1 carrot, cut to fit juicer
1 clove garlic
½ handful parsley
5ml (1 teaspoon) cornflour

225g (8oz) broccoli florets
15ml (1 tablespoon) sunflower oil
50g (2oz) unsalted cashew nuts
450g (1lb) chicken breast fillet, thinly sliced
100g (4oz) frozen sweetcorn kernels

To serve
15ml (1 tablespoon) freshly chopped parsley

1. Par-boil broccoli in a minimum of boiling water for 3 minutes. Drain.
2. With the motor running, juice the tomatoes, carrot, garlic and parsley. Stir cornflour into juice.
3. Heat oil in a wok or large frying pan. Stir-fry cashew nuts for 1 minute until golden. Remove using a draining spoon and drain on absorbent kitchen paper.

4. Stir-fry chicken for 3–4 minutes, until cooked. Add broccoli, sweetcorn, cashew nuts and prepared juice.
5. Stir-fry for 2–3 minutes until boiling. Serve immediately, sprinkled with the parsley.

Chicken and Walnuts in Grape Sauce

Serves 4

Chicken breasts quickly stir-fried with colourful vegetables and walnuts, finished with a sauce made from fresh grape juice, make an excellent meal for entertaining. Serve with wholewheat pasta and a mixed salad.

Preparation time: 15 mins
Cooking time: 10 mins
Kcals per serving: 258

For the juicer
100g (4oz) black seedless grapes, prepared for juicing
½ handful oregano
175g (6oz) slice melon, cut to fit juicer
30ml (2 tablespoons) soy sauce
5ml (1 teaspoon) clear honey
15ml (1 tablespoon) arrowroot

15ml (1 tablespoon) rape seed oil
40g (1½oz) walnut pieces
450g (1lb) chicken breast fillet, cut into strips
1 onion, finely sliced
3 courgettes, sliced at an angle
2 carrots, cut into matchsticks

1. With the motor running, juice the grapes with the oregano and melon. Stir the soy sauce, honey and arrowroot into the juice until blended. Set aside.
2. Heat the oil in a wok or large frying pan. Briefly fry the

walnuts until toasted. Remove using a draining spoon and blot dry on absorbent kitchen paper.
3. Add chicken and onion to the hot oil. Stir-fry for 3 minutes. Add courgettes and carrots to the pan and stir-fry for a further 3–4 minutes.
4. Stir juice mixture again and pour into pan. Bring to the boil, stirring. Simmer for 1–2 minutes, until sauce thickens slightly.
5. Serve immediately, sprinkled with the toasted walnuts.

Gammon and Chicken Stir-fry
Serves 4

A high fibre, low fat recipe that's quick to prepare and cook. Serve with boiled rice or jacket potatoes.

Preparation time: 15 mins
Cooking time: 10 mins
Kcals per serving: 230

For the juicer (to make the sauce)
1 medium carrot, cut to fit juicer
2 tomatoes, cut to fit juicer
2.5cm (1 inch) slice fresh pineapple with its skin, sliced to fit juicer
½ handful parsley
30ml (2 tablespoons) soy sauce
10ml (2 teaspoons) arrowroot

15ml (1 tablespoon) rape seed oil
225g (8oz) lean gammon, sliced thinly
225g (8oz) chicken breast, cut into thin strips
1 onion, chopped
2 sticks celery, chopped
1 parsnip, grated
1 red pepper, seeded and chopped
100g (4oz) mangetout

To serve
freshly chopped parsley

1. With the motor running, juice the carrot, tomatoes, pineapple and parsley. Set aside.

2. Heat the oil in a wok or large frying pan.
3. Stir-fry the gammon and chicken for 3 minutes, until starting to brown.
4. Add the onion, celery, parsnip and red pepper and stir-fry for a further 3–4 minutes.
5. Add the soy sauce to the juice from the machine with the arrowroot. Stir to blend.
6. Pour the juice and arrowroot mixture onto the vegetables, then add the mangetout. Bring to the boil, stirring. Simmer for 1–2 minutes, then serve immediately.

Oriental Stir-fry
Serves 4

This is an excellent way to make rump steak go a bit further so the calorie count remains low in this delicious main meal dish. Serve with brown rice or boiled noodles.

Preparation time: 10 mins
Cooking time: 5 mins
Kcals per serving: 244

For the juicer
175g (6oz) fresh pineapple, sliced to fit juicer
1 shallot
2 plums, stoned and sliced to fit juicer
10ml (2 teaspoons) arrowroot
60ml (4 tablespoons) soy sauce

15ml (1 tablespoon) olive oil
1 large onion, finely chopped
2 green peppers, seeded and sliced
350g (12oz) rump steak, cut into thin strips
100g (4oz) button mushrooms, sliced
30ml (2 tablespoons) freshly chopped parsley

1. With the motor running, juice the pineapple with the shallot and plums. Blend the arrowroot and soy sauce into the juice and set aside.
2. Heat the oil in a wok or large frying pan. Stir-fry the onions and peppers for 1 minute. Add steak and stir-fry for a further 2–3 minutes.
3. Stir in the mushrooms and stir-fry for a further minute.

4. Pour in juice from the juicer and bring to boil, stirring.
5. Simmer for 1 minute, until slightly thickened, then serve sprinkled with the freshly chopped parsley.

Orange and Lime Stir-fried Beef
Serves 4

Citrus fruits make a refreshing sauce to go with beef which is quickly cooked in this colourful stir-fry. Serve on a bed of noodles.

Preparation time: 15 mins
Cooking time: 8 mins
Kcals per serving: 330

For the juicer
2 oranges, peeled and cut to fit juicer, discarding pips
2 cloves garlic

20ml (1 tablespoon + 1 teaspoon) rape seed oil
450g (1lb) lean rump steak, cut into thin strips
1 medium onion, chopped
1 medium carrot, cut into matchsticks
75g (3oz) mangetout, cut in half at an angle
Salt and freshly ground black pepper

1. With the motor running, juice the oranges with the garlic. Stir the juice and set aside.
2. Heat the oil in a wok or large frying pan.
3. Stir-fry the steak for 2 minutes, until starting to brown.
4. Add the onion and carrot. Stir-fry for a further 2 minutes. Add the mangetout and stir-fry for 2 minutes. Finally add the juice from the juicer and stir until bubbling, 1–2 minutes.
5. Season to taste with salt and pepper and serve immediately.

Vegetable Sauté
Serves 4

This stir-fry recipe is particularly good at Christmas. The fresh cranberries make a delicious, instant sauce using the juicer. Serve on a bed of steaming wholewheat pasta.

Preparation time: 10 mins
Cooking time: 9 mins
Kcals per serving: 120

For the juicer
100g (4oz) fresh cranberries
75g (3oz) seedless black grapes
5ml (1 teaspoon) clear honey
5ml (1 teaspoon) cornflour

450g (1lb) Brussels sprouts, peeled and bottoms cut with a knife
225g (8oz) frozen French dwarf beans
15ml (1 tablespoon) olive oil
450g (1lb) courgettes, sliced
100g (4oz) mushrooms, sliced
1 red pepper, seeded and chopped

To serve
25g (1oz) honey-toasted sunflower seeds

1. Put sprouts and beans into a large saucepan. Add 300ml (10 fl oz) cold water. Cover with a lid and bring to the boil. Simmer for 5 minutes, until just tender. Drain.
2. With the motor running, juice the cranberries with the grapes. Stir in the honey and cornflour to blend and set aside.

3. Heat the oil in a wok or large frying pan. Sauté courgettes and mushrooms for 3–4 minutes. Add red pepper with the drained vegetables.
4. Pour in the juice from the juicer. Bring to the boil, stirring.
5. Serve immediately on a bed of pasta, topped with the sunflower seeds.

Nutty Vegetable Stir-fry
Serves 4

A very quick, healthy way to cook vegetables. Crunchy and delicious, serve this stir-fry with a small portion of grilled chicken, turkey or fish for a speedy main course or just with boiled egg noodles. Sukiyaki sauce is available from leading supermarkets, but if you can't find it, use soy sauce instead.

Preparation time: 10 mins
Cooking time: 6 mins
Kcals per serving: 210

For the juicer
175g (6oz) melon, cut to fit juicer
½ handful oregano
1 × 100g (4oz) eating apple, cut to fit juicer

15ml (1 tablespoon) rape seed oil
350g (12oz) cabbage, shredded
350g (12oz) courgettes, sliced
1 red pepper, seeded and diced
225g (8oz) fresh beansprouts
225g (8oz) button mushrooms, sliced
50g (2oz) pine nuts
60ml (4 tablespoons) sukiyaki sauce
10ml (2 teaspoons) arrowroot

1. With the motor running, juice the melon with the oregano and apple. Set aside.
2. Heat the oil in a wok or large frying pan, then add the cabbage and courgettes. Stir-fry for 2–3 minutes.

3. Add red pepper, beansprouts and mushrooms and stir-fry for a further 2 minutes. Stir in pine nuts.
4. Stir sukiyaki sauce and arrowroot into juice, until blended. Add to pan.
5. Cook, stirring, for a further 2 minutes, until boiling and slightly thickened.
6. Serve immediately.

Prawn Provençale
Serves 4

King prawns quickly stir-fried with fresh vegetables, then served with a Provençale sauce made easily on the juicer is simply delicious. Present this tasty meal on a bed of boiled brown rice or wholewheat noodles.

Preparation time: 10 mins
Cooking time: 10 mins
Kcals per serving: 158

For the juicer (to make the sauce)
½ handful fresh parsley
½ stick celery, cut to fit juicer
4 tomatoes, cut to fit juicer
2 cloves garlic
1 red pepper, cut to fit juicer
4 spring onions, cut to fit juicer
100g (4oz) red or black seedless grapes, prepared for juicing
A little salt and freshly ground black pepper
30ml (2 tablespoons) tomato purée

15ml (1 tablespoon) rape seed oil
1 small aubergine, diced
2 courgettes, diced
1 red pepper, seeded and chopped
1 medium carrot, cut into matchsticks
16 raw king prawns, peeled and de-veined
15ml (1 tablespoon) cornflour

To serve
freshly chopped oregano

1. Make the sauce. With the motor running, juice the parsley and celery with the tomatoes, garlic, red pepper, spring onions and grapes.
2. Season the juice with a little salt and pepper and stir in the tomato purée. Set aside.
3. Put aubergine and courgettes into a colander. Sprinkle with salt and set aside for 15 minutes. Rinse well under cold running water, then drain.
4. Heat the oil in a wok or large frying pan and when really hot, stir-fry the aubergine and courgettes for 2 minutes. Add the red pepper and carrot and continue to stir-fry for a further 2 minutes.
5. Add the prawns and stir-fry until pink, 2 minutes.
6. Blend the cornflour with a little water in a small mixing bowl, then pour the juice into the bowl and blend again until smooth.
7. Pour sauce into wok. Bring to the boil, stirring, and simmer for 1–2 minutes, until slightly thickened.
8. Serve immediately, sprinkled with freshly chopped oregano.

Main Meals

Tuna and Avocado with Pasta

Serves 4

A hearty pasta dish that's filling yet low in calories. Serve with a green salad.

Preparation time: 15 mins
Cooking time: 15 mins
Kcals per serving: 330

For the juicer
1 onion, cut to fit juicer
½ handful parsley sprigs
1 clove garlic
1 stick celery

300ml (10 fl oz) passata
Salt and freshly ground black pepper
200g (7oz) can tuna in brine, drained and flaked
½ small, ripe avocado, peeled and diced
225g (8oz) dried pasta shapes
50g (2oz) reduced fat Cheddar cheese, grated
50g (2oz) white breadcrumbs

1. With the motor running, juice the onion with the parsley, garlic and celery.
2. Turn the passata into a medium size saucepan. Stir in the juice from the juicer. Season with a little salt and pepper. Bring to simmering point, stirring, then cover and simmer for 5 minutes. Flake tuna and add to the pan with the avocado. Simmer for a further 5 minutes.
3. Meanwhile, cook the pasta in a large pan with plenty of boiling, salted water until *al dente*, according to

directions on the packet. Drain and turn into a large ovenproof dish. Set aside.
4. Pre-heat the grill to medium hot.
5. Add the tomato sauce to the pasta and mix well.
6. Sprinkle with grated cheese and breadcrumbs. Grill until golden. Serve immediately.

Halibut with Dill and Parsley Sauce

Serves 4

Fish baked in citrus juice with tomatoes, until meltingly tender, then served with a creamy sauce made from low-fat ingredients is extremely satisfying and tasty yet low in calories. Serve with pasta or rice and carrots or courgettes.

Preparation time: 10 mins
Cooking time: 22 mins
Kcals per serving: 173

For the juicer
½ orange, peeled and sliced to fit juicer, discarding pips
1 small wedge lime, peeled
1 tomato, sliced to fit juicer
2 sprigs parsley
Salt and freshly ground black pepper

4 × 175g (6oz) halibut or cod steaks

For the sauce
25g (1oz) low-fat spread
25g (1oz) plain flour
150ml (5 fl oz) fish or vegetable stock
30ml (2 tablespoons) freshly chopped parsley
5ml (1 teaspoon) wholegrain mustard

1. Pre-heat the oven to 200°C (400°F) gas mark 6.
2. With the motor running, juice the orange with the lime, tomato and parsley. Season with a little salt and pepper.

3. Arrange fish in a single layer in a shallow ovenproof dish. Remove the foam from the juice by scooping it off with a spoon, then pour the juice over the fish.
4. Cover the dish with foil and bake in the oven for 15–20 minutes or until just cooked. (Fish should flake easily and no longer appear opaque.)
5. Lift fish with a fish slice onto serving dish. Cover and keep warm.
6. To make the sauce, place low-fat spread, flour, stock and juices from the fish into a saucepan. Bring to the boil over a moderate heat, stirring continually, preferably with a balloon whisk. Simmer for 1–2 minutes until sauce thickens. Remove from heat and stir in parsley and mustard. Adjust seasoning.
7. Serve the fish with the sauce poured over.

Marinated Salmon
Serves 4

Fresh salmon is always a treat, especially for slimmers as it's low in calories. Serve this tasty fish dish with boiled rice or egg noodles and salad. Sukiyaki sauce is available from leading supermarkets but if you can't find it, use soy sauce instead.

Preparation time: 10 mins
Cooking time: 8 mins
Kcals per serving: 180

For the juicer (to make the marinade)
1 clove garlic
1 celery stalk, cut to fit juicer
2 medium size tomatoes, cut to fit juicer
½ handful parsley
1 eating apple, cut to fit juicer
15ml (1 tablespoon) sukiyaki sauce
10ml (2 teaspoons) olive oil

4 fresh salmon cutlets

1. Make the marinade. With the motor running, juice the garlic, celery, tomatoes, parsley and apple, then blend in the sukiyaki sauce and the olive oil.
2. Put the salmon in a single layer in a shallow dish. Pour the marinade over. Cover and set aside for 2 hours, or chill in the fridge overnight, turning the fish in the marinade once or twice.
3. When ready to serve, lift fish from marinade and

barbecue or grill until just cooked, turning occasionally. Serve immediately.

Cod Steaks in Lime Marinade

Serves 4

A low-fat dish which is surprisingly filling when served with boiled rice or pasta and a salad.

Preparation time: 10 mins + marinating time
Cooking time: 10 mins
Kcals per serving: 142

For the juicer
½ lime, peeled and sliced to fit juicer, discarding pips
½ handful tarragon
75g (3oz) green seedless grapes
Salt and freshly ground black pepper
10ml (2 teaspoons) olive oil

4 cod steaks

1. With the motor running, juice the lime with the tarragon and grapes. Stir the juice, then stir in a seasoning of salt and pepper with the olive oil.
2. Arrange the cod steaks in a single layer in a shallow dish.
3. Pour over the juice mixture. Cover with cling film and set aside for 30 minutes or refrigerate overnight.
4. When ready to serve, pre-heat the grill to medium hot. Lift the cod from the marinade and arrange on grill rack. Grill for 8–10 minutes, turning occasionally until fish flakes easily and is no longer opaque (don't over-cook). Serve immediately.

Juicy Beef Casserole

Serves 4

Let the juicer take the headache out of preparing some of the vegetables for this tasty casserole. A full flavoured dish, serve with jacket potatoes, boiled brown rice or pasta.

Preparation time: 15 mins
Cooking time: 2½ hours
Kcals per serving: 262

For the juicer
3 tomatoes, sliced to fit juicer
1 courgette, sliced to fit juicer
1 stick celery, cut to fit juicer
1 wedge lemon, peeled, discarding pips
½ handful fresh parsley

450g (1lb) lean casserole beef, cubed
15ml (1 tablespoon) flour
Salt and freshly ground black pepper
15ml (1 tablespoon) olive oil
1 large onion, chopped
2 medium size carrots, diced
225g (8oz) swede, diced
1 parsnip, diced
175ml (6 fl oz) beef stock

To serve
freshly chopped parsley

1. Juice the tomatoes with the courgette, celery, lemon and parsley. Stir juice and set aside.

2. Toss the beef in the seasoned flour to coat evenly. (This is easiest done by putting beef, flour and seasoning in a plastic bag and shaking.)
3. Heat the oil in a large casserole dish, then add the onions and carrots and sauté for 5 minutes, until starting to soften. Remove from heat.
4. Add the swede, parsnip and the beef. Pour over the juice from the juicer and the stock. Season with a little salt and pepper.
5. Bring to the boil, stirring.
6. Cover with a lid and simmer gently for 2–2½ hours, until meat and vegetables are tender. Stir once or twice during this time.
7. Serve immediately, sprinkled with finely chopped parsley.

Bolognese Sauce
Serves 4

A quickly made sauce that's full of flavour. Serve with wholewheat spaghetti, jacket potatoes or boiled brown rice and plenty of salad.

Preparation time: 10 mins
Cooking time: 35 mins
Kcals per serving: 300

For the juicer
1 clove garlic
1 medium onion, sliced to fit juicer
1 medium carrot, sliced to fit juicer
¼ handful parsley sprigs
¼ green pepper, sliced to fit juicer

450g (1lb) extra lean raw minced beef
397g (14oz) can chopped tomatoes
60ml (4 tablespoons) tomato purée
150ml (5 fl oz) red wine
Salt and freshly ground black pepper
100g (4oz) button mushrooms, sliced

1. With the motor running, juice the garlic with the onion, carrot, parsley and green pepper. Set aside.
2. Dry-fry the beef in a medium size non-stick pan until starting to brown.
3. Stir in the juice from the juicer, the tomatoes with any juice, tomato purée and the red wine. Season with a little salt and pepper.

4. Bring to the boil, cover with a lid and simmer for 30 minutes. Stir in the mushrooms and continue to simmer for a further 10 minutes. Serve immediately.

Chicken in Plum and Orange Sauce

Serves 4

Succulent chicken cooked in juice with stock and garlic makes a deliciously warming lunch or suppertime treat. Serve with steaming pasta or jacket potatoes.

Preparation time: 15 mins
Cooking time: 1 hour 20 mins
Kcals per serving: 265

For the juicer
2 cloves garlic
3 plums, sliced to fit juicer, discarding central stone
1 medium orange, peeled and sliced to fit juicer, discarding pips

15ml (1 tablespoon) olive oil
1 carrot, sliced
1 onion, chopped
8 boneless chicken thighs, skinned
2 medium size red peppers, seeded and chopped
150ml (5 fl oz) dry white wine
1 chicken stock cube
2 bay leaves
20ml (4 teaspoons) cornflour
175g (6oz) mangetout, trimmed
15ml (1 tablespoon) freshly chopped parsley

1. With the motor running, juice the garlic with the plums and orange. Stir and set aside.

2. Heat the oil in a large, flame-proof casserole.
3. Sauté the carrot and onion for 5 minutes.
4. Add the chicken to the dish, then sprinkle over the chopped peppers. Pour in the juice from the juicer and the wine. Add the stock cube and the bay leaves.
5. Bring to the boil then reduce heat, cover and simmer for 1 hour.
6. Mix the cornflour to a smooth paste with a little water and stir into the casserole with the mangetout. Simmer for a further 15 minutes, stirring occasionally. Remove the bay leaves.
7. Serve the casserole sprinkled with parsley.

Classic Coq au Vin
Serves 4

When you have time to relax and cook something traditional, enjoy this well-flavoured classic French dish. Serve with brown rice or wholemeal pasta and French beans.

Preparation time: 10 mins
Cooking time: 1 hour 10 mins
Kcals per serving: 390

15ml (1 tablespoon) olive oil
4 chicken thighs, skinned
4 small part-boned chicken breasts, skinned
75g (3oz) lean gammon bacon, diced
15 shallots, dipped into boiling water, then peeled
225g (8oz) button mushrooms, halved
20ml (1 tablespoon + 1 teaspoon) flour

For the juicer
4 tomatoes, cut to fit juicer
1 small eating apple
1 stick celery, cut to fit juicer
2 cloves garlic

300ml (10 fl oz) red wine
30ml (2 tablespoons) freshly chopped parsley

1. Heat the oil in a heavy based casserole. Sauté the chicken pieces until golden brown on all sides, turning frequently, about 10 minutes. Remove using draining spoon and set aside.

Main Meals

2. Add bacon and shallots to casserole and sauté until browned.
3. Return chicken to casserole, add mushrooms and sprinkle over flour.
4. With the motor running, juice the tomatoes, apple, celery and garlic.
5. Gradually stir juice from the juicer into casserole with the wine.
6. Cook, stirring continually, until sauce boils and thickens. Stir parsley into the sauce.
7. Cover and simmer gently for 45 minutes until chicken is tender.
8. Serve immediately.

Chicken Parcels in Tomato Sauce

Serves 4

Tender breast of chicken with a cheese and garlic filling served with a fresh tomato sauce – a delicious lunch or supper good enough for entertaining. Serve with new potatoes and a mixed salad.

Preparation time: 15 mins
Cooking time: 30–35 mins
Kcals per serving: 255

4 × 150g (5oz) chicken breast fillets, skinned
100g (4oz) low-fat soft cheese with garlic and herbs
15ml (1 tablespoon) arrowroot
Salt and freshly ground black pepper
15ml (1 tablespoon) tomato purée
150ml (5 fl oz) chicken stock

For the juicer
3 medium size tomatoes, sliced to fit juicer
½ medium onion, sliced to fit juicer
1 stick celery, cut to fit juicer
1 small wedge lime, peeled
1 eating apple, sliced to fit juicer
½ handful parsley or oregano

To serve
30ml (2 tablespoons) freshly chopped parsley

1. Pre-heat the oven to 200°C (400°F) gas mark 6.
2. With a wooden rolling pin, beat each chicken breast flat

(rather like you would beat a rump steak) so that they are approximately 1.25cm (½ inch) thick.
3. Spread 25g (1oz) of the cheese onto each breast and roll up, like a Swiss roll.
4. Arrange the chicken breasts in a shallow dish keeping the join underneath and securing with wooden cocktail sticks if necessary.
5. Cover the dish with foil and roast for 30–35 minutes, until chicken is tender.
6. Meanwhile, prepare the sauce. With the motor running, juice the tomatoes with the onion, celery, lime, apple and parsley or oregano.
7. Turn juice into a small pan. Blend the arrowroot with a little water and stir into the pan. Season with salt and pepper and stir in the tomato purée and stock.
8. Bring to the boil, stirring. Simmer for 1–2 minutes, until slightly thickened.
9. Serve the chicken breasts cut into slices with the tomato sauce poured over, sprinkled with freshly chopped parsley.

Turkey Chinese-Style
Serves 4

A marinade is used to soak poultry, meat or fish before cooking to make it more tender. The juicer provides a wonderful method of making instant marinades and sauces from prime fresh ingredients. Serve the turkey with jacket or new potatoes cooked in their skins and a mixed salad.

Preparation time: 10 mins
Cooking time: 20 mins
Kcals per serving: 240

For the juicer (to make the marinade)
1 clove garlic
¼ medium onion, sliced to fit juicer
½ handful oregano
100g (4oz) fresh pineapple, cut to fit juicer
15ml (1 tablespoon) soy sauce
10ml (2 teaspoons) rape seed oil

4 turkey breast fillets, skinned

1. With the motor running, juice the garlic with the onion, oregano and pineapple. Stir the soy sauce and rape seed oil into the juice.
2. Arrange the turkey breasts in a single layer in a shallow dish. Pour over the marinade.
3. Cover and refrigerate for 2–4 hours, or overnight, turning the turkey in the marinade once or twice.
4. Lift the turkey from the marinade and cook under a pre-heated grill, turning fairly frequently until cooked, about 20 minutes.
5. Serve immediately.

Marinated Leg of Lamb with Ginger

Serves 6

Lean leg of lamb marinated overnight for tenderness then roasted until meltingly tender makes a delicious Sunday meal, and is also ideal for entertaining. Serve with jacket potatoes and a selection of vegetables.

Preparation time: 10 mins + marinating time
Cooking time: 1 hour 40 mins
Kcals per 100g (4oz) serving: 180

For the juicer (to make the marinade)
5mm (¼ inch) piece fresh root ginger
1 stick celery, cut to fit juicer
2–3 sprigs celery leaves
1 clove garlic
¼ medium onion
1 lemon, peeled and sliced to fit juicer (first remove rind with a zester)
½ handful coriander leaves
15ml (1 tablespoon) olive oil
Salt and freshly ground black pepper

1.75kg (4lb) leg of lamb
2–3 sprigs rosemary

1. Make the marinade. With the motor running, juice the ginger, celery, celery leaves, the garlic, onion, lemon and coriander.

2. Stir juice and add the olive oil with a seasoning of salt and pepper and the lemon rind.
3. Put the lamb into a shallow dish. Pour marinade over. Cover and refrigerate overnight, basting and turning the lamb in the marinade two or three times.
4. When ready to cook, pre-heat the oven to 190°C (375°F) gas mark 5. Lift lamb from marinade and put into a roasting dish. Place rosemary on top of lamb.
5. Roast for 25 minutes per 450g (1lb), or until the juices run clear when lamb is pierced with a skewer. Cover with foil if lamb becomes over brown.
6. Allow lamb to rest for 15 minutes then carve.

Lamb with Pears
Serves 4

For a quick and easy casserole that tastes as though you spent hours peeling and chopping vegetables, try this lamb dish. Serve with rice or pasta.

Preparation time: 15 mins
Cooking time: 1 hour 5 mins
Kcals per serving: 390

For the juicer
1 large onion, cut to fit juicer
1 carrot, cut to fit juicer
2 Williams pears, quartered
½ handful coriander or parsley
1 parsnip, cut to fit juicer

15ml (1 tablespoon) rape seed oil
450g (1lb) lean braising lamb, cubed
15ml (1 tablespoon) plain flour
1 lamb stock cube
2 bay leaves
Salt and freshly ground black pepper
100g (4oz) baby sweetcorn, halved
2 courgettes, sliced

1. Heat oil in a large flameproof casserole. Toss lamb in seasoned flour and stir into the oil. Fry for 3–4 minutes, until sealed.
2. With the motor running, juice the onion with the carrot, pears, coriander and parsnip. Stir into casserole. Add

stock cube, bay leaves and seasoning of salt and pepper. Bring to the boil, stirring.
3. Cover with a lid and simmer gently for 1 hour, adding a little extra water if casserole becomes dry. Remove any scum which may have formed. Remove the bay leaves.
4. Add baby sweetcorn and courgettes. Simmer, covered, for a further 15 minutes then serve.

Scalloped Roots with Bacon

Serves 6

This filling meal is cooked in one pot so it saves on the washing-up. Serve with a mixed leaf salad for a family lunch or supper.

Preparation time: 15 mins
Cooking time: 1¼–1½ hours
Kcals per serving: 200

750g (1½lb) potatoes, peeled and thinly sliced
1 large onion, chopped finely
225g (8oz) parsnips, peeled and thinly sliced
225g (8oz) carrots, peeled and thinly sliced
225g (8oz) turnips, peeled and thinly sliced
1 stick celery, thinly chopped
175g (6oz) lean gammon, diced
Salt and freshly ground black pepper
300ml (10 fl oz) chicken or vegetable stock
50g (2oz) half-fat Cheddar cheese, grated
5ml (1 teaspoon) mild paprika

For the juicer
2 medium size tomatoes, sliced to fit juicer
½ handful celery leaves
1 small size lemon, peeled

1. Pre-heat the oven to 190°C (375°F) gas mark 5.
2. Seasoning as you go, layer the vegetables with the bacon into a gratin dish, starting and ending with a layer of potatoes and overlapping the vegetables slightly.
3. With the motor running, juice the tomatoes with the

celery and lemon. Mix resulting juice into the stock and pour over vegetables.
4. Cover with foil and bake for 1¼–1½ hours until vegetables are tender.
5. Remove foil. Increase heat to 220°C (425°F) gas mark 7.
6. Sprinkle cheese and paprika evenly over vegetables. Return to oven and bake for a further 10–15 minutes until top is golden. Serve immediately.

Herby Omelette with Mushrooms

Serves 4

Omelettes are fast to cook and filling, too. Use the juicer for speed and efficiency to produce a fresh-tasting omelette that's full of flavour. Serve with a salad.

Preparation time: 5 mins
Cooking time: 10 mins
Kcals per serving: 191

For the juicer
1 onion, sliced to fit juicer
2 medium tomatoes, sliced to fit juicer
½ handful mixed herbs (parsley, thyme, oregano, chives, marjoram)

6 eggs, size 2
Salt and freshly ground black pepper
30ml (2 tablespoons) sunflower oil
225g (8oz) mushrooms, sliced (a mixture of button, oyster and chestnut if possible)
225g (8oz) mozzarella cheese, thinly sliced

1. With the motor running, juice the onion with the tomatoes and herbs.
2. Break the eggs into a large mixing bowl. Whisk with a fork or electric whisk, then beat in the juice from the juicer. Season with a little salt and pepper.
3. Heat oil in a large frying pan, add mushrooms and sauté for 3–4 minutes, until softened. Pour in the egg mixture

and cook for about 8 minutes over a medium heat until the omelette loosens from the pan and is almost set.
4. Top with slices of mozzarella and place under a preheated grill to finish cooking and brown the cheese. Serve immediately.

Salads and Vegetable Dishes

Tomato, Kidney Bean and Sugar Snap Salad

Serves 4–6

This crisp pretty salad is quick to put together and very popular so make it on a regular basis. Full of vitamins with plenty of fibre and a delicious flavour, this is a useful salad for most occasions.

Preparation time: 10 mins
Cooking time: 5 mins
Kcals per serving: 118 for 4, 79 for 6

For the juicer
1 × 100g (4oz) Cox's apple, sliced to fit juicer
¼ lemon, peeled and sliced to fit juicer, discarding pips

225g (8oz) sugar snap peas, topped and tailed
225g (8oz) cherry tomatoes, halved
1 stick celery, chopped
220g (7½oz) can kidney beans, drained and rinsed

For the dressing
5ml (1 teaspoon) wholegrain mustard
Salt and freshly ground black pepper
5ml (1 teaspoon) olive oil
5ml (1 teaspoon) dried oregano

1. With the motor running, juice the apple and the lemon. Set aside.
2. Bring a small pan of water to the boil. Add the sugar snap peas. Simmer for 3–4 minutes, then drain and

immediately refresh under cold running water. Put into a mixing bowl.
3. Add tomatoes, celery and red kidney beans to the bowl.
4. Make the dressing. Add the mustard, a seasoning of salt and pepper, the olive oil and oregano to the juice from the juicer. Whisk briefly with a fork. Pour over salad vegetables and toss to coat.
5. Turn into serving dish and serve immediately.

Radicchio, Sweetcorn and Spinach Salad with Bacon

Serves 4

A small amount of grilled back bacon makes this salad particularly appealing without adding too many calories. Serve on the buffet table or with chicken or fish dishes.

Preparation time: 15 mins
Cooking time: 5 mins
Kcals per serving: 144

2 rashers lean back bacon, rinded
175g (6oz) frozen sweetcorn kernels
100g (4oz) radicchio, shredded (or red cabbage)
225g (8oz) fresh young spinach leaves
100g (4oz) alfalfa sprouts, washed

For the juicer
1 clove garlic
1 medium size carrot, cut to fit juicer
1 spring onion, cut to fit juicer
1 Cox's apple, sliced to fit juicer
Salt and freshly ground black pepper

1. Grill the bacon until crisp, drain on absorbent kitchen paper to remove excess fat, then snip into small pieces and set aside.
2. Cook the sweetcorn in a minimum of boiling water according to directions on the packet. Drain immediately and refresh under cold running water. Drain and put into a large salad bowl.

Salads and Vegetable Dishes

3. Add the radicchio to the bowl then prepare the spinach. Pull any coarse stalks off the spinach and discard. Wash the spinach in several changes of cold water. Drain well, pat dry with absorbent kitchen paper and tear into bite size pieces. Add to salad bowl. Add alfalfa sprouts and bacon.
4. With the motor running, juice the garlic with the carrot, onion and apple. Season to taste with salt and pepper.
5. Stir juice from juicer, pour over salad ingredients, toss to coat and serve immediately.

Salads and Vegetable Dishes 159

Fruity Salad
Serves 4

A colourful combination of vegetables tossed in a tangy dressing. Excellent for entertaining.

Preparation time: 10 mins
Cooking time: 5 mins
Kcals per serving: 60

100g (4oz) broccoli spears, divided into tiny florets
½ Iceberg lettuce, shredded
100g (4oz) cherry tomatoes, halved
5cm (2 inch) piece cucumber, diced
½ ripe avocado
50g (2oz) seedless black or green grapes

For the juicer
1 tomato, sliced to fit juicer
½ apple
1 spring onion, cut to fit juicer
1 clove garlic
5ml (1 teaspoon) wholegrain mustard
Salt and freshly ground black pepper

To serve
freshly chopped parsley

1. Simmer the broccoli in the minimum of boiling water until tender-crisp, about 4 minutes. Drain through a sieve then refresh under cold running water until cold. Drain well and turn into a mixing bowl.
2. Add the lettuce, tomatoes and cucumber to the bowl.

3. With the motor running, juice the tomato with the apple, spring onion and garlic. Stir the juice and whisk in the mustard with a seasoning of salt and pepper.
4. Add the avocado and grapes to the bowl. Pour over the juice from the juicer. Toss to coat and serve immediately, sprinkled with the parsley.

Mushroom, Sweetcorn and Celery Salad with Blue Cheese Dressing

Serves 4

Mushrooms are wonderfully nutty sliced raw then mixed with other ingredients to make a tasty salad.

Preparation time: 10 mins
Cooking time: 5 mins
Kcals per serving: 135

100g (4oz) frozen sweetcorn kernels
100g (4oz) button mushrooms, sliced
3 large sticks celery, finely chopped
25g (1oz) raisins

For the juicer
½ handful chives
1 small stick celery, cut to fit juicer
2 small wedges lemon, peeled, discarding pips
1 clove garlic
1 spring onion, cut to fit juicer
3 broccoli florets

45ml (3 tablespoons) plain, thick set, low-fat yoghurt
50g (2oz) Stilton or Roquefort cheese, grated
Salt and freshly ground black pepper

1. Cook the sweetcorn in boiling salted water until just tender, according to directions on the packet. Drain through a sieve then refresh under cold running water. Drain well and turn into a mixing bowl.

2. Add mushrooms, celery and raisins to the bowl.
3. With the motor running, juice the chives with the celery, lemon, garlic, spring onion and broccoli.
4. Turn the yoghurt into a clean, medium size mixing bowl. Stir in the juice from the juicer until blended. Add the blue cheese. Mix well then season to taste with a little salt and pepper.
5. Pour the dressing over the salad. Toss to coat then serve immediately.

Crispy Salad with Lemon and Tarragon Dressing

Serves 4

Well flavoured and deliciously crisp to eat, this salad goes down well on the buffet table or can be served with pizzas, jacket potatoes or almost any meal.

Preparation time: 10 mins
Cooking time: 0
Kcals per serving: 84

For the juicer
½ lemon, peeled and sliced to fit juicer, discarding pips
¼ medium onion, cut to fit juicer
½ stick celery, cut to fit juicer

150ml (5 fl oz) natural yoghurt
5ml (1 teaspoon) clear honey
2.5ml (½ teaspoon) grated lemon rind
15ml (1 tablespoon) freshly chopped tarragon
Salt and freshly ground black pepper
2 eating apples, 1 green skinned and 1 red skinned if possible
1 large stick celery, chopped
75g (3oz) red cabbage, finely shredded
1 small yellow pepper, seeded and diced
75g (3oz) beansprouts
25g (1oz) pecan nuts, chopped

1. Prepare the dressing. With the motor running, juice the lemon with the onion and celery. Turn the yoghurt into a mixing bowl. Blend in the juice from the juicer and the

honey, lemon rind and tarragon. Season to taste with a little salt and pepper. Set aside.
2. Core and roughly chop the apples, and put into a large mixing bowl.
3. Add the celery, cabbage and yellow pepper. Put the beansprouts into a colander. Stand colander in the sink and pour over a kettle full of boiling water. Drain, then refresh under cold running water.
4. Drain well and add to the bowl. Add the pecan nuts.
5. Pour prepared dressing over salad. Toss well to coat. Turn into serving dish and serve immediately.

Salads and Vegetable Dishes

Special Rice Salad
Serves 4

A useful vegetable dish that's excellent on the buffet table – colourful, filling and tasty.

Preparation time: 10 mins
Cooking time: 15 mins
Kcals per serving: 115

100g (4oz) easy-cook brown rice
½ red pepper, seeded and chopped
100g (4oz) cherry tomatoes, halved
175g (6oz) broccoli florets
30ml (2 tablespoons) freshly chopped parsley

For the juicer
3 medium size tomatoes, sliced to fit juicer
1 large stick celery, cut to fit juicer
Small wedge lime, peeled, discarding pips
8 fresh coriander leaves
1 clove garlic
30ml (2 tablespoons) olive oil
Salt and freshly ground black pepper
5ml (1 teaspoon) Dijon mustard

To serve
50g (2oz) chopped pistachio nuts

1. Cook the rice according to directions on the packet. Drain through a sieve then rinse with plenty of cold water. Drain well and turn into a large mixing bowl. Blot dry with absorbent kitchen paper.

2. Add red pepper to the rice with the tomatoes.
3. Cook the broccoli in boiling, salted water for 3–4 minutes until just cooked and still retaining some bite. Drain and rinse with cold water. Drain and add to the rice.
4. Prepare the dressing. With the motor running, juice the tomatoes with the celery, lime, coriander and garlic. Stir the olive oil into the juice and a seasoning of salt and pepper. Whisk in the mustard.
5. Fork the parsley into the salad. Turn into a serving dish and serve, sprinkled with the pistachio nuts. Serve immediately.

Salads and Vegetable Dishes

Slimmers' Coleslaw
Serves 4

Colourful red and green cabbage with carrots in a juicy dressing – this attractive salad dish will be popular with everyone.

Preparation time: 15 mins
Cooking time: 0
Kcals per serving: 95

175g (6oz) red cabbage
175g (6oz) green cabbage
3 sticks celery
2 medium size carrots
Zest of ½ orange
75g (3oz) seedless grapes
85ml (3 fl oz) natural low-fat yoghurt
30ml (2 tablespoons) reduced calorie mayonnaise

For the juicer
1 spring onion
½ orange, peeled and sliced to fit juicer, discarding pips
½ stick celery
½ handful parsley sprigs
Salt and freshly ground black pepper

To serve
1 large ripe tomato

1. Finely shred the red and green cabbage, discarding any outside leaves and central core.
2. Put cabbage into a large mixing bowl. Finely chop the

celery and add to the bowl. Grate the carrots and add to the bowl with the orange zest and the grapes.
3. With the motor running, juice the spring onion with the orange, celery and parsley. Season the juice with a little salt and pepper.
4. Turn the yoghurt into a mixing bowl. Gradually blend in the mayonnaise with the juice. Adjust seasoning to taste.
5. Pour dressing over cabbage ingredients. Toss to coat. Chop tomato, discarding core.
6. Turn onto a serving dish and serve immediately, topped with the tomato.

Salads and Vegetable Dishes

Microwaved Turnips and Carrots in Apple Juice

Serves 4

Vegetables cooked in apple juice with a little ginger taste sensational. This is a quick and easy recipe that goes well with most main meal dishes.

Preparation time: 10 mins
Cooking time: 8 mins
Kcals per serving: 45

350g (12oz) carrots, cut into matchsticks
225g (8oz) turnips, cut into matchsticks
15g (½oz) low-fat spread

For the juicer
1 Cox's apple, cut to fit juicer
6mm (¼ inch) piece fresh root ginger

To serve
freshly chopped parsley

1. Put the carrots and turnips into a 1.2 litre (2 pint) microwaveable dish.
2. With the motor running, juice the apple with the ginger. Pour over vegetables.
3. Cover the dish with microwave cling film or a lid, and microwave on 100%/FULL power for approx. 8 minutes, stirring and re-covering once, halfway through cooking.

4. Stir in low-fat spread and allow to stand for 2–3 minutes before serving sprinkled with the freshly chopped parsley.

Broad Beans with Courgettes and Cumin
Serves 4

Cumin is a plant of the carrot family native to Egypt, Asia and the Mediterranean region. The spicy seeds are used in curries, sauces, breads and pilaff. Serve this spicy vegetable dish with meat, poultry or fish or just with eggs for a quick veggie meal.

Preparation time: 10 mins
Cooking time: 14 mins
Kcals per serving: 90

For the juicer
1 medium size Cox's apple, sliced to fit juicer
3 sprigs fresh mint
3 plums, sliced to fit juicer, discarding stones
5ml (1 teaspoon) arrowroot

350g (12oz) frozen broad beans
15ml (1 tablespoon) olive oil
1 red skinned onion, peeled and sliced
2 cloves garlic, crushed
2 courgettes, sliced
2.5ml (½ teaspoon) ground cumin
Salt and freshly ground black pepper

To serve
tiny sprigs fresh mint

1. Cook the broad beans in boiling salted water according

to directions on the packet. Drain and set aside.
2. Prepare the juice. With the motor running, juice the apple with the mint and plums. Stir in arrowroot and set aside.
3. Heat the oil in a large frying pan. Add the onion and garlic and sauté for 2–3 minutes, until softened.
4. Stir in the courgettes and fry, stirring, until just starting to brown. Stir in the cumin and cook for a further minute.
5. Season with a little salt and pepper, then stir the prepared juice into the pan. Cover and simmer for 5 minutes.
6. Serve immediately, garnished with the sprigs of mint.

Glazed Vegetable Medley
Serves 4

A colourful trio of vegetables in a well-flavoured glaze.

Preparation time: 5 mins
Cooking time: 12 mins
Kcals per serving: 134

225g (8oz) broccoli spears
225g (8oz) baby courgettes, halved
225g (8oz) baby sweetcorn
25g (1oz) low-fat spread
5ml (1 teaspoon) honey
Salt and freshly ground black pepper
2.5ml (½ teaspoon) dried dill

For the juicer
1 small orange, peeled and sliced to fit juicer, discarding pips
Small wedge lime
1 medium size tomato

1. Steam the vegetables until just tender. This will take about 8–10 minutes. If you don't possess a steamer, simmer the vegetables in the minimum of boiling water until just tender. Drain.
2. Meanwhile, with the motor running, juice the orange with the lime and tomato.
3. Put low-fat spread and honey into a medium saucepan. Add juice from the juicer and a seasoning of salt and pepper. Add dill.

4. Add steamed vegetables. Heat for 1–2 minutes, until boiling.
5. Serve vegetables with the buttery juices poured over.

Aubergine Fiesta
Serves 4

This easy aubergine dish is bursting with flavour and is a great slimmer's dish, as only a little oil is used in the recipe. Toast the sesame seeds briefly under a pre-heated grill before sprinkling over the finished fiesta with the cheese.

Preparation time: 25 mins
Cooking time: 30 mins
Kcals per serving: 150

For the juicer
2 medium size carrots, sliced to fit juicer
1 × 100g (4oz) eating apple, sliced to fit juicer
½ stick celery
2 cloves garlic

1 medium size 275g (10oz) aubergine, diced
3 medium size courgettes, sliced
15ml (1 tablespoon) olive oil
1 large onion, chopped
30ml (2 tablespoons) vegetable purée
5ml (1 teaspoon) dried oregano
1–2.5ml (¼–½ teaspoon) hot chilli powder
Salt and freshly ground black pepper
400g (14oz) can chopped tomatoes
100g (4oz) button mushrooms, chopped

To serve
15ml (1 tablespoon) sesame seeds, toasted
25g (1oz) half-fat Cheddar cheese, grated

1. Put the aubergine and courgettes into a colander. Sprinkle liberally with salt and set aside for 20 minutes, then rinse well under cold running water (this will get rid of the bitter juices). Drain thoroughly and blot dry with absorbent kitchen paper.
2. With the motor running, juice the carrots with the apple, celery and garlic. Stir the juice and season with a little salt and pepper. Set aside.
3. Heat the oil in a large, flameproof casserole, add the onion with the aubergine and courgettes. Cook gently, stirring frequently for 10 minutes, until softened.
4. Remove from heat. Add the vegetable purée, oregano, chilli powder, a seasoning of salt and pepper and the canned tomatoes. Make the juice from the juicer up to 300ml (10 fl oz) with water and add to the casserole. Stir well.
5. Bring to the boil, stirring occasionally. Cover and simmer for 20 minutes.
6. Stir in mushrooms and simmer for a further 5–10 minutes, stirring occasionally, until vegetables are tender.
7. If mixture seems a little wet, remove lid and boil briskly for a few minutes to drive off excess moisture.
8. Serve immediately sprinkled with the toasted sesame seeds and the grated cheese.

Swede and Orange Purée

Serves 4

Swede tastes wonderful with orange juice and parsley; it looks pretty, too, sprinkled with freshly chopped coriander. Delicious with roast turkey, pheasant, chicken or goose.

Preparation time: 10 mins
Cooking time: 32 mins
Kcals per serving: 85

1kg (2lb) swede, peeled and diced
1 vegetable or chicken stock cube
Salt and freshly ground black pepper
30ml (2 tablespoons) freshly chopped parsley
25g (1oz) half-fat soft cheese

For the juicer
2 oranges
1 clove garlic
8 coriander leaves

To serve
freshly chopped coriander

1. Put the swede into a large saucepan. Just cover with cold water. Add the stock cube.
2. Cover with a lid and bring to the boil, stirring once or twice to ensure stock cube dissolves. Simmer for 25–30 minutes, until tender.
3. Meanwhile, remove rind from half of one orange using a zester and reserve.

Salads and Vegetable Dishes

4. Peel both oranges, removing pith, then slice to fit juicer, discarding pips.
5. With the motor running, juice the oranges with the garlic and coriander.
6. Drain the cooked swede and reserve the cooking liquid for a soup or sauce.
7. Mash swede, then beat in juice from juicer with a wooden spoon. Fold in reserved rind. Season to taste with salt and pepper and stir in the parsley and cheese.
8. Return pan to moderate heat and cook, stirring, for 1–2 minutes until thoroughly hot. Serve immediately, sprinkled with the coriander.

Vegetable Purée with Cheese

Serves 4

This delicious vegetable dish is surprisingly filling and sustaining. Serve it with a mixed salad and wholemeal bread for a speedy lunch or supper.

Preparation time: 10 mins
Cooking time: 14 mins
Kcals per serving: 110

350g (12oz) parsnips, peeled and diced
350g (12oz) carrots, peeled and diced
1 celery stalk, chopped
5ml (1 teaspoon) ready-made English mustard
50g (2oz) half-fat Cheddar cheese, grated

For the juicer
2 medium size tomatoes, cut to fit juicer
1 celery stalk, cut to fit juicer
½ handful parsley sprigs

To serve
few snipped chives

1. Put the prepared parsnips, carrots and celery into a mixing bowl. Add 45ml (3 tablespoons) water.
2. Cover with cling film and microwave on 100%/FULL power for 10–12 minutes, until just tender. Stir once halfway through. Allow to stand, covered, for 5 minutes.
3. With the machine running, juice the tomatoes with the celery and parsley.
4. After standing time, turn vegetables with any liquid into

a food processor. Add mustard and juice from the juicer.
5. Process until a smooth purée results, stopping machine once and scraping ingredients from sides, if necessary.
6. Remove blade and fold in grated cheese. Turn into a microwaveable serving dish.
7. Cover with microwave cling film and microwave on 100%/FULL power for 1–2 minutes to reheat.
8. Serve immediately, sprinkled with a few freshly snipped chives.

Desserts

Ice Cream Shake
Serves 2

Peaches combine well with kiwi fruit to produce this creamy shake which can be served as a special snack or dessert. Plenty of food value without too many calories.

Preparation time: 5 mins
Cooking time: 0
Kcals per serving: 78

For the juicer
2 ripe peaches, sliced to fit juicer, discarding central stone
2 kiwi fruit

350ml (12 fl oz) ice cold skimmed milk
2 scoops diet ice cream

To serve
4 strawberries, sliced

1. With the motor running, juice the peaches with the kiwi fruit.
2. Put the juice, milk and ice cream into the food processor.
3. Process until blended.
4. Pour the shake into two tumblers, top with the strawberries and serve immediately.

This recipe makes approximately 720ml (24 fl oz) milk shake.

Blackcurrant and Strawberry Sorbet

Serves 4

This summery sorbet makes an ideal refreshing dessert that's fairly low in calories. Serve with fresh raspberries for an extra special pud.

Preparation time: 15 mins + freezing time
Cooking time: 8 mins
Kcals per serving: 120

75g (3oz) caster sugar
350g (12oz) strawberries, hulled and halved
1 egg white, size 2
15ml (1 tablespoon) icing sugar, sieved

For the juicer
225g (8oz) blackcurrants, prepared to fit juicer
Wedge of lemon, peeled, discarding pips

1. In a medium saucepan, dissolve the sugar in 250ml (8 fl oz) water over a low heat, stirring continuously. Gradually bring to the boil and boil for 3 minutes, without stirring. Set aside to cool completely.
2. With the motor running, juice the blackcurrants with the lemon.
3. Put the strawberries into the food processor. Pour over the juice from the juicer. Process until puréed. Remove blade and stir in the cold sugar syrup until blended.
4. Pour into a plastic freezer container. Cover and freeze until half-frozen.

5. In a clean bowl, whisk the egg white until standing in soft peaks, then whisk in the sieved icing sugar.
6. Whisk in the semi-frozen strawberry mixture, a little at a time, until smooth. Return mixture to freezer container.
7. Freeze until set.

Mango Fool with Strawberries
Serves 4

Mangoes are becoming increasingly popular in the UK. This large tropical fruit has a flavour somewhere between peach and plum, with a yellowy orange flesh. Ripe mangoes 'give' slightly when squeezed, rather like avocados.

Preparation time: 10 mins
Cooking time: 0
Kcals per serving: 100

For the juicer
½ orange, peeled and cut to fit juicer, discarding pips
6 large strawberries, halved
2 sprigs fresh mint

1 large ripe mango, peeled and roughly chopped, discarding central stone
15ml (1 tablespoon) clear honey
150g (5oz) creamy fromage frais
100g (4oz) strawberries, sliced

1. With the motor running, juice the orange with the strawberries and mint.
2. Put the mango flesh into the food processor. Add the juice from the juicer. Process until a smooth purée results.
3. Remove blade and fold in honey and fromage frais.
4. Divide the purée between four sundae dishes or wine glasses.
5. Chill until ready to serve. Serve each dessert topped with a few sliced strawberries.

Fromage Frais Fool
Serves 4

Low-fat fromage frais blended with fruit juice and served with chopped apple tastes alarmingly calorific, yet is kindly low in calories.

Preparation time: 10 mins
Cooking time: 0
Kcals per serving: 79

250g (9oz) fromage frais
1 × 100g (4oz) Cox's apple, cored and roughly chopped
1 banana, sliced, 75g (3oz) peeled weight

For the juicer
100g (4oz) fresh pineapple, cut to fit juicer
½ orange, peeled and cut to fit juicer, discarding pips

To serve
10ml (2 teaspoons) runny honey
a little ground cinnamon

1. Put the fromage frais into a mixing bowl.
2. With the motor running, juice the pineapple and the orange. Stir the juice into the fromage frais.
3. Fold apple and banana into the dessert and divide between four sundae dishes. Serve immediately, drizzled with the honey and dusted with a little cinnamon.

Lemony Apple Snow
Serves 4

A filling dessert that is refreshingly light on the palate. An ideal slimmer's pud that's high on taste and a pretty pink colour to serve.

Preparation time: 15 mins
Cooking time: 8 mins
Kcals per serving: 100

For the juicer
175g (6oz) seedless black grapes
Slice lemon

450g (1lb) Bramley apples, peeled, cored and sliced
25ml (1 tablespoon + 2 teaspoons) caster sugar
Grated rind ½ lemon
2 egg whites, size 3

To decorate
50g (2oz) seedless black grapes, halved

1. With the motor running, juice the grapes with the lemon.
2. Put the apple slices into a medium saucepan. Pour over the juice. Simmer, covered, until apples soften and fall. Remove from heat. Beat to a purée, adding sugar. Set aside to cool completely.
3. Fold lemon rind into purée.
4. In a clean bowl, whisk egg whites until they stand in soft peaks. Using a metal spoon, fold egg whites into fruit purée.
5. Turn into individual dishes and chill until ready to serve.
6. Serve, decorated with the halved grapes.

Desserts

Fresh Fruits with Grand Marnier
Serves 6

Deliciously refreshing and very easy to prepare. An ideal dessert for entertaining.

Preparation time: 10 mins
Cooking time: 0
Kcals per serving: 150

2 pink grapefruits
4 oranges
100g (4oz) strawberries, sliced

For the juicer
1 sharon fruit, sliced to fit juicer
1 orange, peeled and sliced to fit juicer, discarding pips
75g (3oz) seedless grapes, prepared for the juicer
30ml (2 tablespoons) Grand Marnier

To serve
tiny sprigs fresh mint

1. Carefully peel the grapefruit and oranges, removing all skin and pith, holding the fruit over a bowl as you peel to catch any drips of juice.
2. Segment the grapefruit and oranges, without membrane. Put segments into a shallow serving dish. Add the sliced strawberries.
3. With the motor running, juice the sharon fruit with the orange and grapes. Stir Grand Marnier into juice.

4. Pour juice over fruit, cover with cling film and chill in the fridge for at least 20 minutes before serving. Serve decorated with sprigs of mint.

Red Fruit Salad

Serves 4

Summer fruits look like sparkling jewels in this pretty, high fibre fruit salad which has its own natural fruit sauce. Serve the dessert solo or with a little yoghurt, half-fat cream or reduced fat ice cream for a special treat.

Preparation time: 10 mins
Cooking time: 0
Kcals per serving: 107

For the juicer
1 pink grapefruit, peeled and sliced to fit juicer, discarding pips
2 large plums, cut to fit juicer, discarding stones
100g (4 oz) slice fresh pineapple, with skin, cut to fit juicer
30ml (2 tablespoons) white rum
Grated rind ½ orange

225g (8oz) strawberries, halved
225g (8oz) raspberries
10ml (2 teaspoons) caster sugar
100g (4oz) dark red cherries, stoned

1. With the motor running, juice the grapefruit with the plums and pineapple. Stir in the rum and the orange rind.
2. Put the strawberries and raspberries into an attractive bowl, sprinkling the sugar over as you go. Add the cherries.
3. Pour the prepared juice over the fruits. Mix gently to coat then chill until ready to serve.

Spiced Bramleys in Grape Juice
Serves 4

Apples poached in fresh grape juice with a little wine are sensational. Serve with Greek yoghurt. Look for the 6% fat variety (30 kcals per tablespoon) rather than the more readily available 10%.

Preparation time: 5 mins
Cooking time: 10 mins
Kcals per serving: 151

3 cloves
1 cinnamon stick
120ml (4 fl oz) medium sweet wine or cider
25g (1oz) caster sugar
450g (1lb) Bramley apples, peeled, cored and sliced
6 dried apricots (no-need-to-soak variety), quartered
10ml (2 teaspoons) clear honey, or to taste

For the juicer
175g (6oz) black seedless grapes, prepared to fit juicer
175g (6oz) orange, peeled, removing pith and sliced to fit juicer, discarding pips

To serve
60ml (4 tablespoons) 6% Greek yoghurt

1. Put the cloves and cinnamon stick into a medium saucepan. Pour over the wine or cider. Add the sugar.
2. With the motor running, juice the grapes and the orange. Pour into pan, bring to the boil, stirring. Boil for 2–3 minutes to reduce a little.

3. Add the apples and dried apricots to the hot liquid.
4. Cover and simmer gently until fruit is tender, about 4–5 minutes. Remove from heat and taste. Stir in honey to taste, if required.
5. Transfer to a bowl and serve either warm or cold with yoghurt, but don't forget to remove cinnamon stick and cloves on serving!

Jamaican Bananas
Serves 4

This quick and easy dessert really does have the taste of far away, exotic places. Serve with low-fat fromage frais or a little low-fat ice cream.

Preparation time: 5 mins
Cooking time: 5 mins
Kcals per serving: 63

For the juicer
1 large orange, peeled and sliced to fit juicer, discarding pips
½ Cox's apple, sliced to fit juicer
1 small wedge lime, peeled
1–2.5ml (¼–½ teaspoon) ground allspice
30ml (2 tablespoons) rum
5ml (1 teaspoon) demerara sugar

4 small ripe bananas
4 dried apricots, chopped

To serve
low-fat fromage frais or low-fat ice cream

1. With the motor running, juice the orange with the apple and lime.
2. Stir allspice, rum and sugar into juice.
3. Peel bananas, halve lengthways, then cut each half into two pieces. Place in a frying pan in a single layer. Add the dried apricots.

4. Pour over juice from juicer. Heat over a gentle heat until bananas soften, about 5 minutes.
5. Serve immediately with low-fat fromage frais or ice cream.

Baked Apples
Serves 4

Cooking apples baked in fruit juice make a lovely hot but simple dessert that's full of fruity flavour. Serve with plain yoghurt or a little custard made with skimmed milk and half the normal amount of sugar.

Note: I found the baked apples sweet enough following the recipe exactly. Those with a sweet tooth may want to spoon 5ml (1 teaspoon) clear honey into the apple as they break it open to eat. One teaspoon will add 27 kcals.

Preparation time: 10 mins
Cooking time: 40–45 mins
Kcals per serving: 129

For the juicer
3 × 100g (4oz) Cox's apples, sliced to fit juicer
½ orange, peeled and sliced to fit juicer, discarding pips

4 medium size Bramley apples
40g (1½oz) raisins
5ml (1 teaspoon) olive oil

1. Pre-heat the oven to 190°C (375°F) gas mark 5.
2. With the motor running, juice the Cox's apples and the orange. Remove the head from the juice by scooping it off with a spoon and discard, then pour juice into a shallow baking tin.
3. Wash and core the Bramley apples using an apple corer, then with a sharp knife cut a circle round the centre of the apple just breaking the surface of the skin. Cut the bottom from the cores and use as a bung for the base of each apple.

Desserts

4. Stand the apples upright in the baking tin. Fill centres with raisins then brush the tops with a little olive oil.
5. Bake the apples for about 40–45 minutes or until tender, basting them three or four times with the juice during cooking to prevent raisins drying out.
6. When the apples are cooked, lift them on to a serving dish and pour the hot juice over. Serve immediately.
7. Alternatively, if you have a microwave stand the filled apples in a suitable non-metallic dish. Brush tops with a little olive oil. Pour over prepared juice. Cover loosely with microwave cling film. Microwave on power 7 or ROAST for 7–10 minutes. Allow to stand for 3 minutes. Spoon juice over apples and serve immediately.

Melon with Strawberries
Serves 2

This luxurious dessert is excellent for a special dinner *à deux*.

Preparation time: 5 mins
Cooking time: 0
Kcals per serving: 110

1 Ogen melon
100g (4oz) strawberries, sliced
15ml (1 tablespoon) Kirsch

For the juicer
100g (4oz) seedless white grapes, prepared for juicer

To decorate
wedges of lime

1. Halve the melon and remove and discard seeds.
2. Scoop out melon flesh and dice, or use a melon baller. Put flesh with any resulting juice into a large mixing bowl.
3. Add strawberries to the bowl.
4. With the motor running, juice the grapes. Stir Kirsch into juice and pour over fruit.
5. Return melon to shells, cutting edges into an attractive pattern if you have time; alternatively put fruit into two sundae dishes.
6. Serve immediately, garnished with lime.

Pears with Fruity Sauce
Serves 4

This speedy dessert is delicious on a hot summer's day. Add the pears just before serving so they don't discolour.

Preparation time: 10 mins
Cooking time: 3 mins
Kcals per serving: 84

For the juicer
1 apple, sliced to fit juicer
100g (4oz) strawberries, prepared for juicer
1 medium size orange, peeled and sliced to fit juicer, discarding pips

10ml (2 teaspoons) arrowroot
10ml (2 teaspoons) clear honey
2 ripe pears, Williams if possible
100g (4oz) strawberries, sliced
Sprigs of fresh mint

1. With the motor running, juice the apple with the strawberries and orange.
2. Blend arrowroot and honey into juice and transfer to a medium size saucepan.
3. Bring to the boil, stirring. Simmer until slightly thickened. Remove from heat.
4. Pour a pool of sauce onto each of four side plates. Set aside to cool.
5. Peel and halve pears. Carefully remove core.
6. Arrange one pear half in the centre of each pool of sauce.

7. Surround each pear with a few sliced strawberries and serve immediately, decorating each dessert with a sprig of mint.

Melon Cocktail

Serves 2

A whole melon contains only about 100 calories so eat them regularly – the nutrient value is excellent, especially the skins which are juiced in this recipe along with pineapple to make a wonderful sauce. Serve with a little Greek yoghurt.

Preparation time: 10 mins
Cooking time: 0
Kcals per serving: 123

2 × 225g (8oz) slices cantaloupe melon
15g (½oz) dried apricots, chopped
15ml (1 tablespoon) Kirsch (optional)
Grated rind ½ lime

For the juicer
175g (6oz) seedless black grapes, prepared to fit juicer

1. Cut melon flesh away from skin. Cut skin to fit juicer, then dice the melon flesh and put it into a serving bowl. Add the apricots.
2. With the motor running, juice the melon skin with black grapes. Stir the juice well. Stir in the Kirsch, if using.
3. Pour juice over melon and apricots. Sprinkle with the lime rind. Cover and set aside for 10 minutes or so for flavours to mingle.
4. Serve with a little Greek yoghurt if liked.

Mixed Fruit Brûlée
Serves 4

Crème fraîche is a delicious, thick, soured cream from France which is fairly low in calories. The fruit base makes a wonderful tart contrast to the sweet crust. This dessert tastes sensational yet doesn't cost you too many calories!

Preparation time: 10 mins
Cooking time: 5–7 mins
Kcals per serving: 196

For the juicer
1 ripe peach, sliced to fit juicer, discarding central stone
50g (2oz) seedless green grapes, prepared for juicer

175g (6oz) strawberries, sliced
100g (4oz) redcurrants, removed from stem
200ml (8 fl oz) carton low-fat crème fraîche
75g (3oz) demerara sugar

To serve
4 small strawberries
4 sprigs fresh mint

1. With the motor running, juice the peaches with the grapes. Stir juice, removing head with a spoon if preferred.
2. Divide strawberries and redcurrants between four ramekins.
3. Pour the juice evenly over the fruit.
4. Spoon over the crème fraîche to cover the fruit completely.

5. Top each dessert with a quarter of the demerara sugar, to cover the crème fraîche. Place under a pre-heated very hot grill for about 5–7 minutes, until sugar melts and caramelises.
6. Allow to cool, then chill in the fridge until ready to serve. The sugar will harden to a delicious caramel.
7. Serve each brûlée decorated with a strawberry cut into a fan and a sprig of fresh mint.

Slimmers' Trifle

Serves 8

This delicious low-fat trifle is best made a day before serving so that the fruity flavour has time to soak into the sponge. Frozen raspberries work well in this dessert.

Preparation time: 15 mins + chill time to set
Cooking time: 0
Kcals per serving: 125

6 trifle sponges
30ml (2 tablespoons) medium sherry
225g (8oz) raspberries
200g (6oz) seedless grapes
150ml (5 fl oz) Greek yoghurt (6% fat variety)
425g (14oz) can low-fat Devon custard
25g (1oz) toasted flaked almonds

For the juicer
100g (4oz) strawberries, halved
100g (4oz) black or green seedless grapes, prepared for juicer

1. Cut the trifle sponges into strips and arrange in the base of a 1.4 litre (2½ pint) serving bowl.
2. Pour sherry evenly over sponges.
3. Arrange raspberries and grapes over sponges.
4. With the motor running, juice strawberries and grapes. Stir juice and pour over fruit.
5. Cover with cling film and leave in the fridge for 15 minutes to chill slightly. Meanwhile, mix yoghurt into custard.

6. Pour custard mixture over the fruit and return to fridge to chill and set. Cover with cling film and leave overnight, if preferred.
7. Just before serving, top with toasted almonds. Serve on its own or with a little low-fat single cream.

Choux Ring with Mango and Strawberries

Serves 8

Choux pastry can be made successfully with low-fat spread. Here, the choux is baked in a ring which is filled with a low-fat creamy filling.

Preparation time: 15 mins
Cooking time: 30 mins
Kcals per serving: 148

For the choux paste
50g (2oz) low-fat spread
65g (2½oz) plain flour, sieved
2 eggs, size 3, beaten

For the filling
300g (10oz) low-fat fromage frais
Grated rind 1 orange
30ml (2 tablespoons) granulated sweetener

For the juicer
1 ripe mango, peeled and cut to fit juicer, discarding central stone

225g (8oz) strawberries, sliced

To serve
a little sifted cocoa powder

1. Pre-heat the oven to 200°C (400°F) gas mark 6.

Desserts

2. Make the choux ring. Put 150ml (5 fl oz) water into a medium size saucepan with the low-fat spread. Heat over a medium heat until the fat melts. Bring to a rapid boil then remove from heat.
3. Tip in the flour, in one go and beat the mixture with a wooden spoon until you have a smooth ball of dough paste that leaves the side of the pan clean.
4. Gradually beat in the eggs until all are incorporated, but leave just enough to brush over the choux ring.
5. Spoon dessertspoons of mixture onto a greased baking sheet so that they touch each other and form an 18cm (7 inch) circle. Brush all over with remaining egg.
6. Bake for 10 minutes, then increase the heat to 220°C (425°F) gas mark 7 and cook for a further 15–20 minutes.
7. Remove from oven and slit in half horizontally. Return both halves to the oven, open side up, and cook for 3–4 minutes, until dry. Cool on a wire rack.
8. Prepare the filling. Put the fromage frais into a mixing bowl. Stir in the orange rind and sweetener, until dissolved.
9. With the motor running, juice the mango and stir the juice into the fromage frais. Fold in the strawberries.
10. When ready to serve, arrange base of choux ring on a serving dish. Spoon prepared filling evenly into ring. Top with choux pastry lid.
11. Sprinkle with a little sifted cocoa powder and serve immediately.

Citrus Cheesecake
Serves 8–10

A tangy dessert that's surprisingly low in calories, but make sure you restrict yourself to only a small slice of the cheesecake. You will need a 20cm (8 inch) springform tin.

Preparation time: 20 mins + chill time to set
Cooking time: 0
Kcals per serving: 130 1/10 slice, 165 1/8 slice

25g (1oz) butter
50g (2oz) ginger biscuits, crushed
75g (3oz) light digestive biscuits, crushed
11g (1/2oz) sachet powdered gelatine
170g (6oz) can evaporated milk, chilled
250g (8oz) carton low-fat curd cheese
50g (2oz) caster sugar
1 egg white, size 2

For the juicer
1 large orange
1 lemon, peeled and cut to fit juicer, discarding pips

To serve
1 large orange

1. Melt the butter in a saucepan over a low heat. Stir in biscuit crumbs.
2. Press into the base of the springform tin. Chill in the fridge.
3. Remove the zest from the orange using a zester or grater. Set aside. Peel and slice orange to fit juicer.

4. With the motor running, juice the orange and the lemon. Pour into a small bowl and sprinkle gelatine over. Set aside for 10 minutes, then stand bowl over a pan of simmering water and stir until gelatine dissolves. Remove from heat.
5. In a clean mixing bowl, whip the chilled evaporated milk until double in volume. Gradually beat in the curd cheese a little at a time, then fold in the zest from the orange, the sugar and the dissolved gelatine. Stir until well mixed.
6. In a clean mixing bowl, whisk the egg white until standing in soft peaks. Fold into mixture.
7. Pour over prepared cheesecake base and chill in the refrigerator until set.
8. Serve the cheesecake decorated with the fresh orange segments.

Super Juice
Diet Plans

Low-fat Diet

Fat is the dieter's enemy – fats provide a concentrated form of energy and have been closely linked with hardening of the arteries and heart disease. Although fat makes many foods more palatable, cutting most fat out of the diet is quite possible and a substantial weight loss usually occurs.

This healthy diet plan should result in a fairly rapid weight loss, so if you're keen to shed an unwanted 3kg (7lb) in a hurry, stick to the week's plan then congratulate yourself at the end and continue with a healthy eating plan for life.

A FEW RULES
- Follow the day's eating plan each day and make a conscious effort not to eat anything after 6.30 p.m.
- Do drink 150ml (5 fl oz) skimmed milk each day or have 1 diet yoghurt or 1 diet fromage frais or 120ml (4 fl oz) natural low-fat yoghurt daily – the calcium these items contain is vitally important.
- Increase exercise. The more you move around the more calories you burn, so get up a little earlier and use the time to jog, swim, do exercises in front of the television, ride a bike, skip, walk briskly, etc. If possible, walk for 20 minutes each day and attend an exercise class at least once each week.
- If you feel hungry, eat fruit or 1 slice wholemeal toast with yeast extract spread or make up any of the vegetable juice recipes in the book.

Day 1

Breakfast
25g (1oz) no-added-sugar muesli with 85ml (3 fl oz) skimmed milk.
1 apple.

Lunch
1 portion vegetable soup on page 101.
2 slices wholemeal bread spread with a little low-fat spread and filled with 75g (3oz) cottage cheese with chives and 1 tomato, sliced.

Supper
1 serving carrot, pineapple and cucumber juice on page 55.
Mexican Salad Mix 75g (3oz) peeled prawns with ½ small ripe avocado, diced, ½ small red pepper, diced, and 2 spring onions. Toss in a little oil-free dressing and serve on a bed of 50g (2oz) boiled brown rice.
1 low-calorie fromage frais.

Day 2

Breakfast
1 serving healthy breakfast shake on page 41.
1 slice wholemeal toast spread with a little low-fat spread and yeast extract spread.

Lunch
150g (5oz) baked beans in tomato sauce served on 50g (2oz) boiled spaghetti or macaroni and 1 sliced tomato.
1 orange.

Supper
1 serving of any vegetable juice from vegetable juice section.
1 portion scalloped roots from the recipe on page 149.
Large leaf salad tossed in a little fat-free dressing.
1 portion spiced Bramleys in grape juice on page 192.

Day 3

Breakfast
½ grapefruit.
2 Weetabix with 85ml (3 fl oz) skimmed milk.

Lunch
Chicken Pitta 1 pitta bread (wholemeal if possible) warmed under the grill, then filled with 50g (2oz) cooked chicken, skinned and chopped, 1 tomato, chopped, 5 cm (2 inch) piece cucumber, chopped, 2 spring onions, chopped, 2 pimento-stuffed olives, halved, 25g (1oz) seedless grapes, halved, all tossed in 10ml (2 teaspoons) oil-free French dressing.
1 orange.

Supper
1 creamy jacket with tuna on page 97 served with side salad made from lettuce, tomatoes, grated carrot and chopped cucumber.
1 serving tangerine and sharon fruit juice on page 17.

Day 4

Breakfast
25g (1oz) no-added-sugar muesli with 1 serving orange, lime and grape juice on page 26 poured over.
1 apple.

Lunch
1 hard-boiled egg topped with 15ml (1 tablespoon) low-fat fromage frais blended with 2.5ml (½ teaspoon) curry powder. Add 25g (1oz) raisins and serve on a bed of shredded lettuce with 1 tomato, sliced, and 1 spring onion, chopped.

Supper
1 serving of any vegetable juice from the vegetable juice section.
175g (6oz) cooked chicken breast fillet, skinned, served with 1 portion mushroom, sweetcorn and celery salad with blue cheese dressing on page 161.
1 large slice melon.

Day 5

Breakfast
40g (1½oz) bran flakes with 85ml (3 fl oz) skimmed milk.

Lunch
1 portion fruity snack on page 79.

Supper
1 serving of any vegetable juice from the vegetable juice section.
1 portion cod steaks in lime marinade on page 133 served with 175g (6oz) jacket potato and steamed broccoli.

Day 6

Breakfast
1 small orange, sliced, and ½ grapefruit, sliced, served with 30ml (2 tablespoons) Greek yoghurt (6% fat variety).

Lunch
1 portion smoked trout salad on page 87.
1 apple.

Supper
1 portion chicken parcels in tomato sauce on page 142 served with 50g (2oz) brown rice, boiled, and steamed carrots.
1 diet fruit yoghurt.

Day 7

Breakfast
25g (1oz) no-added-sugar muesli with 85ml (3 fl oz) skimmed milk.
1 banana.

Lunch
1 serving tomato solo on page 49.
1 portion vegetable purée with cheese on page 179.
1 large leaf salad tossed in a little oil-free dressing.

Supper
75g (3oz) marinated leg of lamb with ginger on page 145 served with boiled cabbage, new potatoes and carrots.
1 diet yoghurt.

Sweet Tooth Diet

A diet often becomes difficult to stick to when no sweet or pud is offered because of the high calorie count, but desserts needn't be taboo as this seven-day diet plan shows.

Instead of feeling deprived because you're dieting, relax and enjoy the new feeling of confidence and well-being that slimming brings once you have stuck to the plan for more than two days. Learn to reward yourself with treats like exotic fruits – mango, passion fruit, sharon fruit, guava and of course bananas are all naturally very sweet and simply delicious. Eaten in moderation, they will all give you a wonderful feeling of self-indulgence without making you feel guilty. Fruit juice, again in moderation, is also another treat which is simple to prepare, delicious to drink and just as uplifting as an alcoholic tipple.

Discover low-fat alternatives that can be used in desserts instead of ingredients such as full milk, cream and butter. Low-fat evaporated milk, skimmed milk, reduced fat cream products such as Shape and Delight are all readily available to help us beat the flab. Make friends with Quark (a low-fat soft cheese that's excellent in cheesecakes), fromage frais and natural yoghurt – most come in varying percentages of fat, e.g. creamy fromage frais is available with a calorie count of 111 kcals per 100g (4 oz), whilst low-fat fromage frais has a calorie count of 47 kcals per 100g (4oz). Diet ice cream in wonderful flavours is another blessing – try Weightwatchers dairy ice cream which has 35 per cent fewer calories than normal dairy ice cream. Each 140ml (2½ fl oz) portion contains only 96 calories, and that's a pretty generous portion by my standards.

Canned custard now comes in low-fat varieties so use this

creamy sauce in fools and on trifles or serve a little poured over fruits poached gently in fruit juice. Learn to enjoy very small portions of certain foods – that way you are still having a treat with a minimal calorie count.

Try to avoid sugar where possible. You may use a little liquid or granulated sweetener such as aspartame (found in Sweetex granules and liquid Canderel) but sweeteners do tend to leave a slightly unpleasant aftertaste in the mouth so you may prefer not to bother. Fruit juices are wonderful instead of sugar as they add natural sweetness and a wonderful fresh taste to desserts such as fools, mousses, etc. Honey is another slightly sweeter alternative to sugar, but remember 5ml (1 teaspoon) contains approximately 30 kcals.

Day 1

Breakfast
1 serving of kiwi, grape and melon juice on page 20.
1 slice wholemeal toast with 10ml (2 teaspoons) low-fat spread and 10ml (2 teaspoons) marmalade (try a low sugar variety).

Lunch
Cheesy Bake 1 × 175g (6oz) jacket potato filled with ¼ coleslaw recipe on page 167, topped with 25g (1oz) reduced fat Cheddar cheese, grated. 1 tomato.
1 sharon fruit.

Supper
1 serving of any vegetable juice from the vegetable juice section.

Glazed Chicken Brush 1 × 175g (6oz) chicken breast fillet (skinned) with 5ml (1 teaspoon) honey blended with 5ml (1 teaspoon) wholegrain mustard. Grill for 10–15 minutes, turning occasionally. Serve with boiled cabbage, grilled tomatoes and 75g (3oz) cooked weight brown rice.
Small carton diet fromage frais.

Day 2

Breakfast
175g (6oz) slice melon.
2 Weetabix served with 120ml (4 fl oz) skimmed milk and 2 dried apricots, chopped.

Lunch
Hummus Dip Buy 75g (3oz) hummus from the deli and serve with carrot, celery and red peppers sticks and 1 pitta bread, wholemeal if possible.
½ recipe mango and tangerine juice on page 30.

Supper
1 portion classic coq au vin on page 140 served with 100g (4oz) new potatoes, leeks and courgettes.
1 portion Jamaican bananas on page 194.

Day 3

Breakfast
2.5cm (1 inch) slice fresh pineapple.
1 boiled egg, size 3, with 1 slice wholemeal toast spread with 5ml (1 teaspoon) low-fat spread.

Sweet Tooth Diet

Lunch
1 portion bolognese sauce recipe on page 136 served on a bed of 50g (2oz) wholewheat spaghetti. Mixed side salad of lettuce, tomatoes, cucumber and spring onion tossed in a little fat-free dressing.
1 portion mango fool with strawberries on page 186.

Supper
1 serving of any vegetable juice from the vegetable juice section.
Herb and Tomato Omelette In a mixing bowl, beat 2 size 3 eggs with 5ml (1 teaspoon) mixed dried herbs, salt and pepper and 30ml (2 tablespoons) water. Heat 5ml (1 teaspoon) olive oil in an omelette pan. Pour in egg mixture. Cook over fairly high heat, easing sides away, until almost set. Chop one tomato and sprinkle over half the omelette. Fold in half and continue to cook until completely set. Serve with ¼ recipe of the coleslaw recipe on page 167.
175g (6oz) slice melon with 6 fresh strawberries.

Day 4

Breakfast
1 serving healthy breakfast shake on page 41.
1 apple.

Lunch
1 serving of any vegetable juice from the vegetable juice section.
Prawn Salad Top a bed of salad leaves with 3 button mushrooms, sliced, and 4 cherry tomatoes, halved. Sprinkle over 10ml (2 teaspoons) no-fat salad dressing and top with 100g (4oz) peeled prawns. Serve with 1 wholemeal bread roll.

1 diet fromage frais.

Supper
1 turkey breast, Chinese-style, see recipe on page 144, served with 100g (4oz) new potatoes, broccoli and 50g (2oz) sweetcorn kernels.
1 orange.

Day 5

Breakfast
1 serving fruit sunburst juice recipe on page 18.
25g (1oz) bran flakes served with 150ml (5 fl oz) skimmed milk.

Lunch
1 portion mushroom, sweetcorn and celery salad with blue cheese dressing on page 161 served with 175g (6oz) jacket potato.
1 orange.

Supper
1 portion halibut with dill and parsley sauce on page 129 served with 50g (2oz) pasta shapes, carrots and cauliflower.
1 portion Jamaican bananas, see page 194.

Day 6

Breakfast
½ grapefruit.
1 boiled egg.
1 slice wholemeal toast spread with 5ml (1 teaspoon) low-fat spread.

Lunch
1 bowl canned consommé soup.
1 × 200g (7oz) grilled trout served with large mixed salad tossed in a dressing made from tomato juice mixed with a little seasoning and 10ml (2 teaspoons) olive oil.
2 scoops blackcurrant and strawberry sorbet, see recipe on page 184.

Supper
1 serving of any vegetable juice from the vegetable juice section.
¼ recipe for ricotta with apple and walnuts on page 83 served with 1 wholemeal pitta bread.
1 portion red fruit salad on page 191.

Day 7

Breakfast
40g (1½oz) unsweetened muesli with ½ recipe pineapple and satsuma juice on page 36 poured over. 15ml (1 tablespoon) Greek yoghurt (6% fat variety).

Lunch
Smoked Salmon Open Sandwich Top 1 large slice wholemeal bread with lettuce leaves, sliced cucumber, sliced tomato. Sprinkle with lemon juice and salt and pepper. Arrange 75g (3oz) smoked salmon on salad and serve with a knife and fork.
1 portion red fruit salad on page 191.

Supper
1 serving of any vegetable juice from the vegetable juice section.

100g (4oz) lean rump or fillet steak, grilled and served with 100g (4oz) new potatoes, green beans and cauliflower and a sauce made by putting 1 small can 230g (8oz) chopped tomatoes with 15ml (1 tablespoon) red wine, a little salt, a few drops Worcestershire sauce and 15ml (1 tablespoon) parsley sprigs into the food processor and processing until smooth. Heat slowly in a small pan until boiling, stirring frequently.
1 diet fruit yoghurt.

Busy Woman's Diet

How easy it is as a busy working woman or mum to find yourself suddenly indulging in a high calorie snack, which may satisfy hunger pangs in the immediate short term, but does almost no good nutritionally and simply leaves you with dreadful feelings of guilt!

Follow this seven-day diet plan specifically designed with you in mind. Use the hints and tips and enjoy a tremendous feeling of achievement as the pounds start to roll off. The recipes are very easy to compile and follow.

HINTS AND TIPS

- Shop after a meal when you're not feeling hungry – you'll be less likely to pop the wrong foods into your trolley.
- Be prepared – plan your meals a few days ahead so there are always low-calorie ingredients in the house.
- Have plenty of low-calorie nibbles ready prepared in the fridge – celery, carrot, apples, radish, melons, tomatoes, etc. are all ideal.
- Cut down on portion size and endeavour to increase your personal intake of salads, vegetables, fruits, wholemeal bread, pasta, rice, etc., and decrease the amount of fat and protein foods on your plate.
- Use any of the vegetable juices as interesting alternatives to snacks. Full of vitamins and minerals, these healthy drinks give you a tremendous lift and help to fill you up.
- Keep slimming targets realistic, aim to lose approximately 3kg (7lb) in the first month and be delighted with that. Don't become despondent if after the first week weight loss slows down – there's always water loss in week 1 which shows up on the scales.

- Reward yourself. Even if you only lose 225g (½lb) a week you are a success, so treat yourself to a bunch of flowers or an item of clothing – whatever suits your fancy (other than fattening foods).
- Don't give up – constantly remind yourself of how much weight you've already lost and don't be tempted to undo the good you've done by eating sinful foods.
- Keep moving – get out and enjoy walking, running, cycling, swimming or whatever grabs you. Fresh air is good for you and even in winter, sunshine triggers the production of vitamin D in our skins which is essential for the absorption of calcium.
- Take time to enjoy your food and be aware of what you're eating – a bolted breakfast and quick snacks on the run don't seem like a meal, so when you do have time to relax you tend to eat more.

Day 1

Breakfast
2 Weetabix with the juice of 1 large orange poured over, topped with 15ml (1 tablespoon) Greek yoghurt (6% fat variety) blended with 5ml (1 teaspoon) clear honey.

Light Meal
1 wholemeal bap filled with 100g (4oz) tuna fish canned in brine, drained and flaked, mixed with 15ml (1 tablespoon) reduced calorie mayonnaise. Sticks of carrot, celery and red pepper.
1 apple or pear.

Main Meal
1 portion of the vegetable soup on page 101.

1 chicken breast, grilled, 100g (4oz) boiled new potatoes in their skins, salad served with a little fat-free dressing.
1 diet fruit yoghurt.

Day 2

Breakfast

1 serving of the orange and pear juice on page 22.
1 piece wholemeal toast served with 5ml (1 teaspoon) low-fat spread and 5ml (1 teaspoon) reduced sugar blackcurrant jam or a little yeast extract spread, such as Marmite.

Light Meal

Large salad topped with 85ml (3 fl oz) plain yoghurt blended with 25g (1oz) crumbled Stilton or Danish blue cheese.
1 piece fresh fruit.

Main Meal

1 serving of any vegetable juice from the vegetable juice section.
1 portion of the cod steaks in lime marinade on page 133 with steamed carrots.
1 wholemeal bread roll.
1 portion of the ice cream shake on page 183.

Day 3

Breakfast

1 serving of the orange, lime and grape juice on page 26.
30ml (2 tablespoons) muesli (no added sugar variety) with 85ml (3 fl oz) skimmed milk.

Light Meal

1 hard-boiled egg, large leaf salad with oil-free dressing and

25g (1oz) chopped walnuts.
1 recipe carrot and tomato juice on page 67.
1 orange.

Main Meal
1 serving of any vegetable juice from the vegetable juice section.
1 portion chicken and walnuts in grape sauce on page 111 served with 1 portion brown rice and 1 tomato, sliced.
1 pear sliced and topped with 25g (1oz) raisins and 1 serving [140ml (2½oz)] reduced calorie vanilla ice cream.

Day 4

Breakfast
1 serving fruit sunburst juice on page 18.
1 granary roll with 5ml (1 teaspoon) low-fat spread and yeast extract spread.

Light Meal
Large mixed salad, shredded lettuce and cabbage, grated carrot, ¼ sliced avocado, watercress, sliced peppers, tomatoes, sprinkled with fat-free French dressing and topped with 75g (3oz) cottage cheese.
1 apple or orange.

Main Meal
1 portion marinated salmon on page 131 served with boiled carrot and courgette sticks and 150g (5oz) jacket potato with 5ml (1 teaspoon) low-fat spread.

Day 5

Breakfast
1 serving any fruit juice from the fruit juice section.
Porridge made with water and served with 15ml (1 tablespoon) single cream and 5ml (1 teaspoon) clear honey.

Light Meal
75g (3oz) smoked mackerel with celery, carrot and pepper sticks and 1 tomato.
1 apple.

Main Meal
1 serving of any vegetable juice from the vegetable juice section.
1 portion of the bolognese sauce recipe on page 136 served on top of 50g (2oz) boiled spaghetti with a mixed leaf salad tossed in a little fat-free dressing.
1 diet yoghurt.

Day 6

Breakfast
1 serving tangerine, pineapple and melon juice on page 39.
1 poached egg on 1 slice wholemeal toast spread with a little low-fat spread.

Light Meal
250ml (½ pint) carton fresh minestrone soup.
1 cottage cheese pocket recipe on page 85.

Main Meal
1 portion gammon and chicken stir-fry on page 113 served with 1 portion boiled noodles.
1 diet fromage frais.

Day 7

Breakfast
2.5cm (1 inch) slice fresh pineapple.
2 slices wholemeal toast spread with a scraping of low-fat spread and 10ml (2 teaspoons) marmalade.

Light Meal
1 creamy jacket with tuna, cooked in microwave if preferred, see recipe on page 97.
Large salad of shredded lettuce, chopped spring onions, chopped tomatoes and cucumber.
1 pear.

Main Meal
1 portion orange and lime stir-fried beef on page 117 served with 1 portion boiled rice and steamed mangetout and courgette sticks or salad.
1 portion red fruit salad on page 191 served with a little Greek yoghurt (6% fat variety).

Vegetarian Diet

Cutting down on fat is the easiest and most painless way of losing weight without really noticing a change of diet. Vegetarians do this naturally as they don't eat meat which is where the rest of us obtain over a quarter of all the fat we eat. Even when prime lean steak or pork is selected, it's surprising just how much fat is hidden away in the tissue.

A vegetarian diet is essentially healthy. Plenty of minerals and vitamins and lots of protein is found in cereals, beans, pulses, bread and vegetables. As long as low-fat dairy produce (which contains just as much protein and vitamins as full-fat varieties) is selected, a switch to a vegetarian diet will almost certainly mean a loss of weight. Another advantage of vegetarian food is that it is high in fibre, so you won't be constipated, and soluble fibre such as you find in oats and bran takes a long time for the body to digest, so you feel fuller for longer periods and don't suffer from hunger pangs either.

Include plenty of vegetable and citrus juices in your vegetarian diet and don't worry about lack of iron because the body's ability to absorb iron is vastly increased by a diet rich in vitamin C. Green leaf vegetables and pulse beans are reasonable sources of iron, as are wholemeal pasta, rice and bread and any breakfast cereal containing bran. Non-vegetarians may like to follow this vegetarian seven-day eating plan to see how they enjoy 'green cuisine'. The diet is based on varied and interesting menus consisting of approximately 1,200 calories per day.

Make sure you have 300ml (10 fl oz) skimmed milk each day.

Day 1

Breakfast

2 slices wholemeal bread with 15g (½oz) low-fat spread and a little yeast extract spread, such as Marmite.
25g (1oz) vegetarian Edam cheese.
1 orange.

Lunch

1 portion lentil and tomato soup on page 103.
50g (2oz) wholemeal pasta topped with boiled courgettes, leeks, broccoli, cauliflower (as much as you like), 1 small can chopped tomatoes, seasoned and heated, and 25g (1oz) flaked almonds toasted under the grill.
1 apple.

Supper

1 serving of any vegetable juice from the vegetable juice section.
Large leaf salad made from lettuce varieties, watercress, chicory, sliced tomato, celery, cucumber, ½ medium ripe avocado diced, 50g (2oz) cooked, drained sweetcorn tossed in 15ml (1 tablespoon) French oil dressing and 1 granary bread roll.
1 portion pears with fruity sauce on page 199 with 30ml (2 tablespoons) natural low-fat yoghurt.

Day 2

Breakfast

25g (1oz) wholegrain cereal such as bran flakes or All Bran served with milk from allowance.
1 serving special breakfast juice on page 42.

Lunch
1 portion nutty vegetable stir-fry on page 120 served on 50g (2oz), uncooked weight, brown rice, boiled.

Supper
2 slices wholemeal toast spread with 5ml (1 teaspoon) low-fat spread and topped with 225g (8oz) can baked beans in tomato sauce and 1 poached egg. 1 tomato.
1 piece fresh fruit (not banana).

Day 3

Breakfast
1 serving fruit sunburst juice on page 18.
225g (8oz) natural low-fat yoghurt with 1 small sliced banana.

Lunch
1 portion vegetable soup on page 101.
Sandwich made from 2 slices wholemeal bread filled with sliced tomato, shredded lettuce and 50g (2oz) cottage cheese.
1 slice melon or fresh pineapple.

Supper
Pasta with Lentils and Mushrooms 50g (2oz) wholemeal pasta topped with 50g (2oz) red split lentils cooked in 450ml (15 fl oz) boiling salted water for 20–25 minutes, then drained. Garnish with 1 onion, chopped and 75g (3oz) button mushrooms, sliced and fried together in 10ml (2 teaspoons) sunflower oil in a non-stick frying pan.
Side salad of lettuce, tomatoes, courgettes, radish, tossed in low-fat salad dressing.

1 portion mango fool with strawberries on page 186.

Day 4

Breakfast
25g (1oz) wholegrain cereal such as bran flakes or All Bran, served with milk from allowance.
1 orange.

Lunch
1 serving tomato solo vegetable juice on page 49.
Salad Medley 1 large plate salad vegetables of choice with 50g (2oz) canned red kidney beans, drained and rinsed, 25g (1oz) sultanas, 25g (1oz) chopped walnuts, 50g (2oz) chopped button mushrooms and 25g (1oz) half-fat vegetarian Cheddar cheese, grated. Serve with a fat-free dressing or just juice 2 tomatoes with half handful of herbs, season with a little salt and pepper and use as a dressing.
1 diet fromage frais.

Supper
1 serving reviving juice on page 48.
1 portion eggs with mushrooms and tomatoes on page 95 served with 2 slices wholemeal toast spread with 10ml (2 teaspoons) low-fat spread.

Day 5

Breakfast
1 serving apple and pear juice on page 28.
2 slices wholemeal bread spread with 10ml (2 teaspoons) low-fat spread and low sugar marmalade.

Lunch
1 portion vegetable sauté on page 118 served on 50g (2oz), uncooked weight, wholemeal macaroni or brown rice. Side salad.
1 diet fruit yoghurt.

Supper
1 serving pineapple salad juice on page 51.
1 cottage cheese pocket on page 85.
1 baked apple on page 196 served with 30ml (2 tablespoons) reduced fat canned custard.

Day 6

Breakfast
225g (8oz) low-fat yoghurt served with 1 slice fresh pineapple, chopped.

Lunch
1 serving green pepper, carrot and sharon fruit juice on page 59.
Large helping of slimmers' coleslaw on page 167 served with 175g (6oz) jacket potato and 25g (1oz) reduced fat vegetarian Cheddar cheese, grated.
1 portion Weightwatchers vanilla ice cream.

Supper
Pasta Salad Cook 50g (2oz) wholewheat pasta shells or spirals in boiling water, until *al dente*. Drain and rinse under cold running water. Drain again and place in mixing bowl. Add 45ml (3 tablespoons) natural low-fat yoghurt with 2 tomatoes, juiced in juicer, ½ red pepper, diced, ½ medium avocado, chopped, and 15ml (1 tablespoon) freshly chopped

parsley. Season with a little salt and pepper. Toss well to coat and sprinkle with 25g (1oz) chopped walnuts before serving on a bed of lettuce leaves.
1 slice melon or 1 passion fruit.

Day 7

Breakfast

1 serving melon, orange and grapefruit trio on page 40.
Grilled mushrooms on toast. Brush 6 button mushrooms with 5ml (1 teaspoon) olive oil, grill until tender. Serve on 1 slice wholemeal toast.

Lunch

1 serving crispy salad with lemon and tarragon dressing on page 163.
1 pitta bread, wholemeal if possible. Warm the pitta under the grill then fill with the salad before serving.
1 orange.

Supper

1 serving tomato, melon and cucumber juice on page 73.
225g (8oz) jacket potato filled with 1 × 225g (8oz) can spaghetti in tomato sauce served with 1 mini corn on the cob, boiled, and 100g (4oz) mangetout.
1 sharon fruit.

Super Soup Diet

Super-convenient soup, whether you make your own or buy a carton or can, is easy to prepare, fills you up, is comforting, warming and sustaining yet will slim you down effortlessly. Follow this seven-day plan, consisting mainly of soup, and watch the pounds roll away.

A FEW RULES
- Follow the day's meals as outlined. In addition to the plan, each day you should have 300ml (10 fl oz) skimmed milk or, if you prefer, two diet yoghurts or diet fromage frais daily instead of the milk.
- You may drink as much mineral water and unsugared tea and coffee (with milk) from your allowance as you like.
- You may eat as much salad and vegetables as you like, e.g. lettuce, cucumber, celery, tomatoes, cabbage, courgettes, red and green peppers, spinach, beansprouts, watercress, etc., but use only oil-free dressing or one of the vegetable juice recipes to serve with them.

Day 1

Breakfast
1 serving sharon fruit and melon juice on page 34.
25g (1oz) fruit and fibre cereal with 120ml (4 fl oz) skimmed milk.

Light Meal
¼ recipe vegetable soup on page 101.
40g (1½oz) wholemeal French bread with 50g (2oz) cottage cheese and 1 tomato.
1 apple.

Main Meal

225ml (½ pint) Covent Garden Soup Co. fresh minestrone soup.
200g (7oz) baking potato, cooked by microwave or conventional oven, topped with 50g (2oz) canned tuna in brine, drained, 50g (2oz) frozen sweetcorn kernels, cooked according to directions on the packet, 30ml (2 tablespoons) low-fat fromage frais and 5ml (1 teaspoon) tomato purée.
1 slice fresh pineapple.

Day 2

Breakfast
1 serving tangerine and sharon fruit juice on page 17.
1 egg, size 3, poached.
1 slice wholemeal toast with 10ml (2 teaspoons) low-fat spread and yeast extract spread.

Light Meal
½ recipe vegetable soup on page 101 with 1 granary bread roll.
1 apple or pear.

Main Meal
½ recipe bouillabaisse on page 99.
2 crumpets spread with a little low-fat spread.
1 serving pineapple and satsuma juice on page 36.

Day 3

Breakfast
1 serving of orange and pear juice on page 22.
1 portion porridge made with water and served with 25ml

(1 fl oz) reduced fat evaporated milk and 5ml (1 teaspoon) demerara sugar.

Light Meal
1 portion onion soup served with 1 wholemeal bap spread with a little low-fat spread.

Onion Soup (Makes 2 portions)
10ml (2 teaspoons) olive oil
2 medium onions, chopped
450ml (15 fl oz) beef stock
30ml (2 tablespoons) freshly chopped parsley
15ml (1 tablespoon) cornflour
Salt and freshly ground black pepper

1. Heat oil in a large saucepan, then sauté onions for 10 minutes, until softened and golden.
2. Add stock and parsley. Bring to the boil, cover and simmer for 30 minutes.
3. Purée in a food processor or liquidiser. Return to pan.
4. Blend cornflour with a little water and stir in to pan with a seasoning of salt and pepper.
5. Return to boil, stirring constantly, simmer for 2 minutes, stirring, then serve.

1 slice fresh pineapple.

Main Meal
¼ recipe lentil and tomato soup on page 103.
Large leaf salad with a little oil-free dressing, topped with 75g (3oz) canned salmon, drained.
1 diet fromage frais.

Day 4

Breakfast
1 orange.
25g (1oz) fruit and fibre cereal with 120ml (4 fl oz) skimmed milk.

Light Meal
225ml (½ pint) New Covent Garden Soup Co. spinach with nutmeg soup.
40g (1½oz) ciabatta bread with 75g (3oz) cottage cheese with chives.

Main Meal
¼ portion vegetable soup on page 101.
½ recipe for slimmers' coleslaw on page 167, topped with 75g (3oz) peeled prawns and 50g (2oz) canned sweetcorn, drained.
1 apple.

Day 5

Breakfast
1 serving fruit sunburst juice on page 18.
2 Weetabix with 120ml (4 fl oz) skimmed milk.

Light Meal
1 packet low-calorie instant soup.
175g (6oz) jacket potato filled with 1 portion of slimmers' coleslaw on page 167, topped with 15g (½oz) chopped walnuts.

Main Meal
Tomato Soup Using the juicer, slice and juice 3 large tomatoes, 1 medium size courgette, 1 stick celery and 1 clove garlic. Pour into a saucepan and add 150ml (5 fl oz) vegetable stock, 100g (4oz) frozen peas and 75g (3oz) frozen sweetcorn. Simmer for 5 minutes. Blend 15ml (1 tablespoon) cornflour to a smooth paste with a little water, add to soup. Simmer, stirring, for 2 minutes then serve with 40g (1½oz) wholemeal bread and 20g (¾oz) cube Danish Blue cheese.
1 large slice melon.

Day 6

Breakfast
1 serving pineapple and satsuma juice on page 36.
1 egg, size 3, boiled or poached.
40g (1½oz) wholemeal bread with 10ml (2 teaspoons) low-fat spread.

Light Meal
1 packet Knorr Stir-and-Serve cream of asparagus soup topped with 15ml (1 tablespoon) grated Parmesan cheese.
1 wholemeal bread roll.
1 orange.

Main Meal
1 portion haddock and sweetcorn chowder served with 1 granary bread roll spread with 10ml (2 teaspoons) low-fat spread.
Haddock and Sweetcorn Chowder (Makes 2 portions)
150g (5oz) cod or haddock fillet
1 medium onion, chopped
100g (4oz) potatoes, diced

1 chicken stock cube
5ml (1 teaspoon) dried mixed herbs
50g (2oz) frozen sweetcorn
Salt and freshly ground black pepper

1. Dice fish and set aside.
2. Put onions, potatoes, chicken stock cube, dried herbs and 450ml (15 fl oz) water into a pan. Bring to the boil, stirring now and again to ensure stock cube has dissolved. Simmer, covered for 20 minutes.
3. Purée soup in a blender or liquidiser. Return to pan with haddock and sweetcorn. Simmer for 4 minutes, until fish is no longer opaque.

Note: The remaining portion should be cooled then refrigerated overnight and used the following day.
1 portion spiced Bramleys in grape juice on page 192 served with 30ml (2 tablespoons) Greek yoghurt (6% fat variety).

Day 7

Breakfast
1 apple.
25g (1oz) fruit and fibre cereal with 120ml (4 fl oz) skimmed milk.

Light Meal
1 portion haddock and sweetcorn chowder.
1 slice wholemeal toast spread with 10ml (2 teaspoons) low-fat spread.

Main Meal
1 sachet Batchelors Mexican Spicy Tomato Cup-a-Soup.

Spanish Salad (Serves 1)
1 tomato, chopped
75g (3oz) red pepper, seeded and chopped
75g (3oz) canned red kidney beans, drained
50g (2oz) frozen peas, cooked and cooled under cold running water
Few drops chilli sauce
15ml (1 tablespoon) oil-free French dressing
½ small avocado, peeled and sliced
25g (1oz) reduced fat Cheddar cheese, grated

1. Put the tomato, red pepper, kidney beans and peas into a mixing bowl.
2. Shake on a few drops of chilli sauce. Add the French dressing. Toss to coat. Pile onto a serving plate.
3. Top with the avocado and grated cheese. Serve immediately.

100g (4oz) grapes.

Anti-cellulite Diet

Follow this diet for seven days and you should lose up to 3kg (7lb).

Cellulite or orange peel skin, usually found around the bottom and thigh areas of women in particular, is thought to be due to hormonal changes which cause toxins to build up in the fat cells. This causes an irritant reaction, resulting in the formation of hard nodules of connective tissue or cellulite.

Health farms will tell you what you already probably know – cellulite is notoriously difficult to shift but most recommend a fasting programme for the first two days of your visit to help to flush and cleanse the system, followed by a low-fat diet. This easy-to-follow programme is designed to cleanse the system and is guaranteed to make you feel wonderful.

As this diet is fairly rigid you should consult your GP before embarking on it, and please note that rigorous exercise is not recommended for the first three days of the diet. Throughout the diet it is very important to drink plenty of mineral water and the juices recommended, and to avoid tea, coffee and other drinks.

Lunch and supper may be reversed, if preferred.

Day 1

Breakfast
1 serving fruit sunburst juice on page 18.
1 glass mineral water.

Anti-cellulite Diet

Lunch
1 pink grapefruit with 2 glasses mineral water.

Supper
1 serving tomato, melon and cucumber juice, see page 73.
Large plate of steamed vegetables such as courgettes, carrots, French beans, runner beans, celery, broccoli, cauliflower, sprouts or mangetout with 2 large tomatoes juiced with small wedges of lemon. Season juice with a little salt and freshly ground black pepper plus some freshly chopped herbs, and pour over vegetables before serving.

Day 2

Breakfast
Orange and Apple Juice with Melon
1 orange, prepared to fit juicer
1 eating apple, prepared to fit juicer
225g (8oz) slice melon, prepared to fit juicer
Juice the fruit and stir juice well. Drink immediately with ice if preferred.

Lunch
1 serving carrot and tomato juice, see page 67.
1 large plate prepared raw salad vegetables such as lettuce of any type, chopped celery, grated carrot, tomatoes, cucumber, spinach, mangetout, sliced red pepper, shredded radicchio, radishes, baby sweetcorn, etc.
1 apple.

Supper
1 serving carrot, pineapple and cucumber juice on page 55.

Large plate of lightly steamed vegetables such as courgettes, parsnips, carrots, swede, cabbage, cauliflower, French beans, etc.
1 piece fresh fruit.

Day 3

Breakfast
1 serving pink grapefruit and kiwi juice on page 25.

Lunch
100g (4oz) cottage cheese with chives.
1 large plate steamed vegetables, as Day 2.
1 apple.

Supper
1 serving of any vegetable juice from the vegetable juice section.
1 portion of the melon with prawns and strawberry dressing on page 89.
150ml (5 fl oz) low-fat natural yoghurt.

Days 4, 5, 6 and 7

Daily allowance of 300ml (10 fl oz) skimmed milk, otherwise drink plenty of water daily.

Breakfast
1 serving of any fruit juice from the fruit juice section.
½ grapefruit (no sugar).
1 carton low-fat natural yoghurt.

Anti-cellulite Diet

Lunch and Supper
1 serving of any vegetable juice from the vegetable juice section.
1 large plateful of steamed vegetables or 1 large plateful mixed salad topped with one of the following:
175g (6oz) grilled chicken breast, without skin
100g (4oz) tuna fish canned in brine, well drained
175g (6oz) steamed cod or halibut or haddock or any oily fish such as mackerel, trout, salmon, grilled or poached
100g (4oz) braised liver
100g (4oz) cottage cheese
2 hard-boiled or poached eggs (but don't select eggs more than twice in one week)

Desserts
1 piece fresh fruit or 150ml (5 fl oz) carton low-fat natural yoghurt.

Exercise Plan
From Day 4 onwards, it is recommended that you either swim for 20 minutes each day or take a 40-minute brisk daily walk.

De-stress Diet

Food can actually help you cope with stress or it can add to it, depending on how you use it. Feeling uptight and unable to cope makes it surprisingly easy to indulge in sugary snacks such as chocolate, chocolate biscuits, doughnuts, peanuts, crisps, etc., in the false belief that these comfort foods will make you feel better. Strangely enough, they do give you an immediate lift as sugar is rapidly absorbed into the blood stream. However, this 'lift' is extremely short-lived and you quickly feel tired again and probably bloated as well.

We are what we eat, but everyone can re-train eating habits at any time during their lives and maintain them more or less, especially as one begins to feel pleased with the new slim outline reflected in the mirror.

The following diet plan is designed to fill you up and give you plenty of energy as you gradually lose weight. You won't suffer from hunger pangs as you'll be eating plenty of complex carbohydrates such as rice and pasta, and lots of fresh fruit and vegetables as well as drinking healthy invigorating juice. You'll soon feel and look more healthy, have more energy and be well on the way to coping with, if not actually beating, the stress in your life. The diet is set out as a weekly plan but you can change days around if you like and should there be a specific lunch or evening meal that you don't actually like, swop the meal for a lunch or supper on a different day.

A FEW DO'S AND DON'TS
- Limit your intake of milk to 250ml (8 fl oz) skimmed per day.
- Avoid alcohol completely if at all possible but if you must indulge, have 3 small glasses of wine or cider per week.

- Restrict eggs to 3 per week.
- Cut out sugar if possible – you'll soon get used to the taste of food without it.
- Cut down on salt which is associated with high blood pressure. As every processed food we eat has a fairly high concentration of salt, it really does pay to leave the salt cellar off the table.
- Drink plenty of mineral water but little, if any, tea or coffee.

Day 1

Breakfast
½ fresh grapefruit.
1 poached egg, size 3, served on 1 slice wholemeal toast spread with a little low-fat spread.

Lunch
1 serving melon, raspberry and grape juice on page 19.
1 portion recipe tomato, kidney bean and sugar snap salad on page 155 served with 175g (6oz) jacket potato and 75g (3oz) tuna fish in brine, drained.
100g (4oz) grapes.

Supper
225g (8oz) white fish poached or grilled and served with boiled peas, courgettes, leeks and a small can chopped tomatoes liquidised or processed to a purée, then heated with a little seasoning and a few dried herbs and served as a sauce.

Day 2

Breakfast
1 serving kiwi, grape and melon juice on page 20.
2 Weetabix with milk from allowance and 25g (1oz) raisins.

Lunch
Coronation Chicken Sandwich Stir 2.5ml (½ teaspoon) curry powder into 45ml (3 tablespoons) natural low-fat yoghurt, then add 75g (3oz) cooked chopped chicken breast and 5ml (1 teaspoon) mango chutney. Stir in 50g (2oz) halved seedless grapes and sandwich between 2 slices wholemeal bread.
1 orange.

Supper
1 serving of any vegetable juice from the vegetable juice section.
1 portion of the bolognese sauce on page 136 served on 50g (2oz) wholewheat spaghetti.
Large leaf salad tossed in a fat-free dressing.

Day 3

Breakfast
Porridge made from 25g (1oz) porridge oats and water, served with a little milk from allowance and 5ml (1 teaspoon) demerara sugar.
1 orange.

Lunch
1 serving of any vegetable juice from the vegetable juice section.
1 cottage cheese pocket on page 85.
1 pear.

Supper
1 portion of herby omelette with mushrooms on page 151.
Large salad of lettuce, tomatoes, cucumber with grated

carrot and diced celery, tossed in oil-free dressing.
1 wholemeal roll with 5ml (1 teaspoon) low-fat spread.
1 diet yoghurt.

Day 4

Breakfast
1 serving special breakfast juice on page 42.
1 natural low-fat yoghurt.
1 small sliced banana.

Lunch
1 portion recipe beef casserole on page 134 served with 75g (3oz) cooked weight brown rice, boiled cabbage and steamed carrots.
1 orange or pear.

Supper
1 serving of any vegetable juice from the vegetable juice section.
225g (8oz) can baked beans in tomato sauce served on 1 slice wholemeal toast.
1 diet fromage frais.

Day 5

Breakfast
1 serving fruit sunburst juice on page 18.
Porridge made as directed for Day 3.

Lunch
1 serving of any vegetable juice from the vegetable juice section.

1 creamy jacket potato with tuna fish on page 97 served with sliced tomatoes and cucumber.

Supper
1 portion vegetable soup on page 101.
Open Sandwich Spread 2 slices wholemeal bread with a little mustard pickle. Top with shredded lettuce, sliced tomato, sliced cucumber and 75g (3oz) cottage cheese.
1 orange.

Day 6

Breakfast
1 serving hurry breakfast shake on page 43, but do not include milk in daily allowance.
1 apple.

Lunch
1 hard-boiled egg served with 1 portion coleslaw recipe on page 167.
1 wholemeal bap spread with a little low-fat spread.

Supper
1 serving of any vegetable juice from the vegetable juice section.
1 portion chicken and cashew stir-fry on page 109 served with 75g (3oz) cooked weight boiled brown rice and grilled tomatoes.
Baked apple on page 196 served with 15ml (1 tablespoon) low-fat fromage frais.

Day 7

Breakfast

25g (1oz) breakfast cereal with 1 small banana, sliced, milk from allowance and 5ml (1 teaspoon) sugar.

Lunch
1 slimmers' cup a soup.
1 slice wholemeal bread topped with 225g (8oz) can spaghetti in tomato sauce.
1 large slice melon.

Supper
1 serving melon, orange and grapefruit trio on page 40.
75g (3oz) lean roast lamb or 100g (4oz) roast chicken, without skin, served with plenty of steamed broccoli, mangetout and carrots and a little gravy made without fat (use instant gravy granules and vegetable water).
1 portion choux ring with mango and strawberries on page 206.

Detoxifying Juice Diet

This diet uses fasting which helps to clear the mind and body. As long as it is not practised for more than two days at a time, fasting can be beneficial to the body, especially after it has been overloaded with a surfeit of rich foods and alcohol, such as around Christmas-time, but make sure that you set aside two days to fast when demands on you are not too great.

Expect to feel bad at the end of the first day as headaches, weakness, stomach pains and feeling listless are normal and are caused by the toxins being expelled from the system. On the second day you will begin to feel better and fitter but you won't really reap the benefit of fasting until a few days later as you progress with a calorie controlled eating plan and begin to feel wonderfully fit and slim!

Day 1

Breakfast
As well as the juice, drink plenty of bottled mineral water as and when required.

Fruit Juice Special
2 Cox's apples, prepared to fit juicer
1 ripe peach, prepared to fit juicer
100g (4oz) seedless grapes, prepared to fit juicer
Juice the fruit and stir juice well. Pour into a tumbler and serve immediately with ice if preferred. Also good diluted with mineral water.

Lunch
Veggie Juice
3 tomatoes, prepared to fit juicer

Detoxifying Juice Diet

5cm (2 inch) piece cucumber, prepared to fit juicer
2 medium carrots, prepared to fit juicer
1 Cox's apple, prepared to fit juicer
Juice the ingredients and stir juice well. Pour into a tumbler with ice if preferred and drink immediately.

Supper
Carrot and Orange Juice
3 medium size carrots, prepared to fit juicer
1 stick celery, prepared to fit juicer
1 large orange, prepared to fit juicer
Juice the ingredients and stir juice well. Pour into a tumbler with ice if preferred and drink immediately.

Day 2

Breakfast
As well as the juice, drink plenty of bottled mineral water as and when required.

Orange, Apple and Melon Trio
1 large orange, prepared to fit juicer
1 Cox's apple, prepared to fit juicer
225g (8oz) slice melon with skin and seeds, prepared to fit juicer
Juice the fruit and stir juice well. Pour into a tumbler with ice if preferred and drink immediately.

Lunch
Celery and Carrot Juice
2 sticks celery, prepared to fit juicer
2 medium size carrots, prepared to fit juicer
1 apple, prepared to fit juicer

Juice the ingredients and stir juice well. Pour into a tumbler with ice if preferred and drink immediately.

Supper
Mango and Apple Juice with Grapes
½ mango, prepared to fit juicer
2 Granny Smith's apples, prepared to fit juicer
100g (4oz) seedless grapes, prepared to fit juicer
Juice the fruit and stir juice well. Pour into a tumbler, with ice if preferred and drink immediately.

For the remaining five days of this diet, follow last five days of the Anti-cellulite Diet on pages 244–7.

Healthy Kids' Diet

It is important that children have a balanced, healthy diet enabling them to form good eating habits which will remain with them for the rest of their lives, so help them eat sensibly.

Good general nutrition means that children do get the necessary foods without much trouble but a few points should be noted:

- Plenty of calcium in childhood and young adult life gives bones a good chance of not becoming brittle in old age when calcium is lost. Calcium is found in milk, yoghurt, cheese, green vegetables, beans, sardines and nuts.
- Protein is used by children to build new tissue as they grow, so ensure they have enough reduced fat cheese and milk, fish, eggs, lean meat, chicken and pulse vegetables such as red kidney beans, baked beans, chick peas, etc. so that they're getting protein without too much fat.
- Cut down on fats, particularly hidden fats in crisps, cakes, pastry, biscuits, etc. It has been proved that a high fat diet in young children leads to heart attacks in later life so you're doing kids a real favour by restricting fatty foods.
- Watch sugar intake – particularly fruit squashes and sweets which tend to coat the teeth with sugar and cause tooth decay and, if taken in sufficient quantity, obesity. Babies do not appreciate sweet foods so don't be responsible for giving your child a sweet tooth.
- Nutritionists recommend children eat more complex carbohydrates, including fibre in place of fat. Grains contain B vitamins so serve plenty of wholemeal bread, brown rice, wholegrain pasta, etc. Potatoes, too, are great

for kids as they have a high proportion of vitamin C and are low in calories.
- Vitamins and minerals are vitally important to children so ensure they have plenty of fresh fruit and vegetables. If they won't eat vegetables, encourage them to drink vegetable juice. Simply play around with the recipes in the vegetable juice section until you find one that suits or make up your own. Remember, a little fruit added with the vegetables will make the juice more palatable. Kids love the carrot, sharon fruit and parsley juice on page 56.

MILK
Whole milk is best for under-fives as they need the extra calories it provides for energy and growth. However, children over the age of two who eat a wide variety of good nutritious foods can switch to semi-skimmed milk which is just as high in all nutrients but lighter on fat.

SNACKS
Try to discourage eating snacks that have high concentrations of sugar and fat; instead offer fresh fruit, fruit and vegetable juices, diet yoghurts and low-fat fromage frais, sticks of carrot and celery, unsweetened biscuits, bread. Unsweetened popcorn with a little grated cheese is popular and different. Kids will only expect biscuits and crisps if they're always in the house, so be brave and stop buying them!

HEALTHY FAST FOODS
When you're pressed for time remember there are plenty of healthy fast foods available. Fresh fruits, raw vegetables, fruit and vegetable juices, wholemeal toast with

Healthy Kids' Diet

eggs or baked beans, microwave jacket potatoes, canned fish, fish fingers grilled without any added fat, diet yoghurts, pasta with low-fat sauces and unsweetened breakfast cereals are all good examples.

A word about the seven-day plan

The diet which follows gives a seven-day healthy eating plan for children. If followed correctly, overweight children will soon lose unwanted pounds without feeling hungry.

Day 1

Breakfast
1 or 2 Weetabix, according to appetite, served with 200ml (7 fl oz) milk and 5ml (1 teaspoon) sugar if really necessary.
1 banana.
1 serving of any fruit juice from the fruit juice section.

Lunch
1 portion juicy beef casserole on page 134 served with boiled potatoes in their skins, cabbage and carrots.
150ml (5 fl oz) carton natural low-fat yoghurt with 25g (1oz) raisins or 1 diet fruit yoghurt.

High Tea
1 serving of any vegetable juice from the vegetable juice section.
225g (8oz) can baked beans on wholemeal toast, spread with a little low-fat spread and sliced or grilled tomatoes.
1 portion citrus cheesecake on page 208.

Day 2

Breakfast
1 serving of any fruit juice from the fruit juice section.
1 boiled egg with 1 slice wholemeal toast spread with a little low-fat spread.

Lunch
225g (8oz) jacket potato filled with 5ml (1 teaspoon) low-fat spread and 75g (3oz) tuna fish in brine or oil, well drained.
Slimmers' coleslaw according to appetite, see recipe on page 167.
1 tomato.
75g (3oz) grapes or 1 apple.

High Tea
1 lean beefburger, well grilled and served in a large wholemeal bap with 15ml (1 tablespoon) tomato relish or tomato sauce but no butter or spread (they won't miss it!).
1 mixed salad including lettuce, grated carrot, sliced cucumber, chopped celery and sliced tomato, served with no more than 15ml (1 tablespoon) salad cream or 15ml (1 tablespoon) reduced calorie mayonnaise.
1 serving of any fruit juice from the fruit juice section.

Day 3

Breakfast
1 bowl puffed wheat cereal with 1 ripe pear, chopped, and 200ml (7 fl oz) milk.
1 serving of any fruit juice in the fruit juice section.

Lunch
Cheese on Toast In a mixing bowl combine 40g (1½oz) grated reduced fat Cheddar cheese or grated Edam with 15ml (1 tablespoon) reduced fat mayonnaise. Spread onto lightly toasted wholemeal bread and grill until golden.
1 portion lemony apple snow on page 188.

High Tea
3 fish fingers, grilled without any added type of fat served with garden peas and a small portion of oven chips.
1 serving of any vegetable juice from the vegetable juice section.
1 apple or slice melon.

Day 4

Breakfast
1 serving of any fruit juice from the fruit juice section.
1 portion muesli (no added sugar variety) served with 200ml (7 fl oz) milk and 1 small apple, chopped.

Lunch
Ham Sandwich 2 slices wholemeal bread spread with a little low-fat spread and 5ml (1 teaspoon) reduced calorie mayonnaise, filled with 50g (2oz) lean ham, 50g (2oz) shredded lettuce and 1 sliced tomato.
1 diet fromage frais or diet yoghurt.

High Tea
1 serving of any vegetable juice from the vegetable juice section.
Baked Fish Wrap 200g (7oz) cod steak in foil with 50g (2oz) frozen sweetcorn kernels, 1 sliced tomato and a seasoning of

salt and freshly ground black pepper. Bake in a moderately hot oven, 200°C (400°F) gas mark 6, for 15 minutes. Serve with 40g (1½oz) boiled brown rice or 175g (6oz) jacket potato with 5ml (1 teaspoon) low-fat spread.
1 piece fresh fruit.

Day 5

Breakfast

1 serving of any fruit juice from the fruit juice section.
1 Shredded Wheat served with 25g (1oz) raisins, 5ml (1 teaspoon) sugar (optional) and 200ml (7 fl oz) milk.

Lunch

1 poached egg served on 150g (5oz) mashed potato, made with semi-skimmed milk but no butter or margarine.
1 portion slimmers' coleslaw on page 167.
1 slice melon.

High Tea

1 portion chicken and cashew stir-fry on page 109 served on 50g (2oz) portion boiled noodles.
1 serving of any vegetable juice from the vegetable juice section.
1 Penguin biscuit.

Day 6

Breakfast

1 serving of any fruit juice from the fruit juice section.
1 or 2 Weetabix, according to appetite, served with 1 small banana and 200ml (7 fl oz) milk and 5ml (1 teaspoon) sugar (optional).

Healthy Kids' Diet

Lunch
1 portion vegetable soup on page 101.
Cheese and Tomato Sandwich Spread 2 slices wholemeal bread with a little low-fat spread, then fill with 50g (2oz) grated reduced fat Cheddar cheese and 1 sliced tomato. Serve with carrot and celery sticks.
1 orange.

High Tea
1 serving of any vegetable juice from the vegetable juice section.
1 portion lamb with pears on page 147 served with pasta shapes and carrots.
1 portion slimmers' trifle on page 204 or 1 piece fresh fruit.

Day 7

Breakfast
1 serving of any fruit juice from the fruit juice section.
1 portion fruit and fibre breakfast cereal served with 200ml (7 fl oz) milk and 5ml (1 teaspoon) sugar (optional).

Lunch
1 portion vegetable purée with cheese on page 179 served with 1 grilled tomato and a few grilled mushrooms.
1 diet yoghurt.

High Tea
1 serving of any vegetable juice from the vegetable juice section.
Salad made with lettuce, tomatoes, grated carrot and cucumber mixed with 25g (1oz) raisins and 15ml (1 tablespoon) fat-free dressing. Serve on a plate topped with 1

or 2 low-fat pork sausages, well grilled and sliced.
1 slice wholemeal bread spread with 5ml (1 teaspoon) low-fat spread.

Pregnancy Plan

From the time of conception, and right through pregnancy is not the time to diet rigidly, but it is the time to follow a highly nutritious eating programme. Stopping smoking, cutting alcohol consumption completely if possible, and revising your diet if necessary are the golden rules for pregnant women.

MILK
You do need about 600ml (1 pint) milk per day but there's no need to have more. Skimmed milk contains all the other nutrients found in whole milk, but far less fat so opt for that.

FRYING
Stop frying foods altogether – it's a messy way of cooking and very fattening so grill, steam or poach foods instead. You'll soon get used to the delicious light, fresh taste.

SUGARY SNACKS
Avoid biscuits, cakes, pies, sugar, etc. Sugar provides nothing but empty calories along with a bit of comfort! Go for freshly made vegetable juices and fresh fruit and vegetables instead, and drink plenty of bottled mineral water too.

PROTEIN
Protein is of vital importance as the body's requirement doubles during pregnancy. As a general guide, make sure you have two helpings daily of one of the following: fish,

lean meat, reduced fat cheese, pulse vegetables, nuts, poultry. Eggs, another high protein food, may be eaten twice a week but no more as they are fairly high in cholesterol.

VITAMINS AND MINERALS

Vitamin C increases the amount of iron absorbed from food and, as iron is vital for the development and growth of the baby, eating iron-rich foods such as meat, liver (but not more than once a week), wholemeal bread, dark green vegetables with a glass of freshly made citrus juice, or with fresh fruit and vegetables high in vitamin C will ensure maximum absorption.

During pregnancy the need for iron and calcium doubles. Try to get this from your diet instead of relying on supplements. Your GP will advise you but remember that freshly made juice delivers the maximum amount of vitamins and minerals from really fresh produce into your blood stream within minutes. The juice from the juicer is so much better than juice in cans, cartons or bottles as it is fresh, is not pasteurised and has absolutely no colourings, flavourings or preservatives added. Fresh fruits and vegetables are bursting with vitamins A, C and K, so aim to have four helpings each day.

FATS

Fats are always the dieter's enemy. Cut down on these for the sake of yourself and the baby. With milk and other dairy foods, select low-fat varieties (this can help prevent morning sickness too). Look for low-fat yoghurt, skimmed milk, low-fat fromage frais and reduced fat cheeses such as quark, cottage cheese and light creamy cheeses.

FIBRE

Eat plenty of fibre-rich foods – bran (also high in zinc), wholemeal bread, brown rice, wholewheat pasta, pulses and fresh fruit and vegetables are all vital parts of the healthy diet. Whole grains (wholemeal bread, brown rice, etc.) are also rich sources of essential vitamin B. Such a diet, along with plenty of water, will make you feel great, and constipation, a plight for many pregnant mums, will become a thing of the past.

WEIGHT GAIN

Doctors vary in advising weight gain expectations but most suggest an increase of about 13kg (28lb) during pregnancy. Be guided by your weight at the start of pregnancy and listen to the nurse at the ante-natal clinic where you are weighed regularly.

The diet which follows gives a seven-day healthy eating plan for pregnant women. It is not aimed to be a weight reduction plan in any way, but simply gives a sensible eating programme, so don't bother to weigh out exact quantities – just follow the broad outline. 600ml (1 pint) skimmed or semi-skimmed milk should be consumed daily but part may be used in cooking (e.g. cauliflower cheese on Day 1).

Day 1

Breakfast
1 serving melon, orange and grapefruit trio on page 40.
1 poached egg.
2 slices wholemeal toast with 15g (½oz) low-fat spread and a little reduced sugar marmalade or jam.

Lunch

Large bowl lentil and tomato soup on page 103.
1 slice wholemeal toast with 15g (½oz) low-fat spread and 50g (2oz) cottage cheese.
150g (5oz) natural low-fat yoghurt with 1 pear.

Supper

1 serving carrot and tomato juice on page 67.
Cauliflower cheese made with 150ml (5 fl oz) semi-skimmed milk and no more than 50g (2oz) reduced fat Cheddar cheese.
175g (6oz) jacket potato.
1 tomato.
1 helping red fruit salad on page 191 served with 1 small scoop Weightwatchers vanilla ice cream.

Day 2

Breakfast

2 Weetabix with 150ml (5 fl oz) milk and 5ml (1 teaspoon) sugar, if necessary.
1 serving plum, raspberry and grape juice on page 33.

Lunch

100g (4oz) smoked trout or smoked mackerel served with large salad including watercress and tomatoes, and a fat-free dressing.
1 wholewheat bread roll spread with 15g (½oz) low-fat spread.
1 orange.

Supper

1 serving carrot, mangetout and broccoli juice on page 72.
1 portion bolognese sauce on page 136 served on 75g (3oz) wholewheat spaghetti.

Tomato and Onion Side Salad Slice 1 or 2 tomatoes into a dish. Add 1 or 2 chopped spring onions and half handful chopped oregano. Sprinkle with 10ml (2 teaspoons) red wine vinegar and season with salt and freshly ground black pepper before serving.

1 diet yoghurt or diet fromage frais.

Day 3

Breakfast
40g (1½oz) All Bran cereal served with 150ml (5 fl oz) milk and 5ml (1 teaspoon) sugar, if necessary.
1 orange.

Lunch
1 serving pink grapefruit and kiwi juice on page 25.
175g (6oz) jacket potato filled with 1 portion slimmers' coleslaw on page 167 and topped with 40g (1½oz) grated reduced fat Cheddar cheese.
200g (7oz) slice melon.

Supper
1 serving tomato solo juice on page 49.
1 portion gammon and chicken stir-fry on page 113 with 75g (3oz) boiled brown rice and small side salad with low-fat dressing.
1 portion mango fool with strawberries on page 186.

Day 4

Breakfast
1 serving special breakfast juice on page 42.
40g (1½oz) Shredded Wheat with 150ml (5 fl oz) milk and 5ml (1 teaspoon) sugar, if necessary.

Lunch

1 cottage cheese pocket on page 85.
1 ripe pear served with 45ml (3 tablespoons) Greek yoghurt (6% fat variety).

Supper

1 helping radicchio, sweetcorn and spinach salad on page 157 served with 1 small chicken portion, skinned and spread with 5ml (1 teaspoon) wholegrain mustard and a few drops lemon juice, then grilled or barbecued for 20–25 minutes, until juices run clear.
175g (6oz) jacket potato.
1 baked apple on page 196 served with 30ml (2 tablespoons) reduced fat canned custard.

Day 5

Breakfast

40g (1½oz) All Bran cereal with 150ml (5 fl oz) milk and 5ml (1 teaspoon) sugar, if necessary.
2 slices wholemeal toast with 15g (½oz) low-fat spread and a little reduced sugar marmalade.
1 orange.

Lunch

1 serving spring vegetable tonic on page 63.
1 portion lamb with pears on page 147 served with 75g (3oz) brown rice, boiled, and green beans and cabbage.
1 peach or pear.

Supper

1 serving tomato, cucumber and pepper juice on page 68.

1 portion herby omelette with mushrooms on page 151 served with 1 portion slimmers' coleslaw on page 167.
1 wholemeal roll.
1 slice melon.

Day 6

Breakfast
1 serving orange and pear juice on page 22.
150g (5oz) baked beans on 1 slice wholemeal toast.

Lunch
1 portion lentil and tomato soup on page 103.
1 portion scalloped roots with bacon on page 149.
1 large leaf salad including lettuce, watercress, celery and shredded cabbage tossed in a little no-fat salad dressing.
1 diet fromage frais.

Supper
1 portion tuna and avocado with pasta on page 127 served with mangetout.
2 scoops blackcurrant and strawberry sorbet on page 184 served with fresh strawberries and 15ml (1 tablespoon) single cream.

Day 7

Breakfast
1 serving orange, lime and grape juice on page 26.
40g (1½oz) Shredded Wheat or Weetabix served with 150ml (5 fl oz) milk and 5ml (1 teaspoon) sugar, if necessary.

Lunch
1 serving carrot and tomato juice on page 67.
1 cod steak or 1 salmon steak, grilled with a little sunflower oil, served with 150g (5oz) new potatoes, boiled in their skins, carrots and broccoli.
1 portion slimmers' trifle on page 204.

Supper
1 portion crispy salad with lemon and tarragon dressing on page 163 served with 75g (3oz) lean ham.
1 apple.

Index

A
Apple
  apple and orange juice 21
  apple and pear juice 28
  baked apples 196
  broccoli, sprout and apple juice 54
  cabbage, tomato and apple juice 65
  carrot, celery and apple juice 52
  ginger, carrot and apple juice with tomato 61
  lemony apple snow 188
  microwaved turnips and carrots in apple juice 169
  orange, apple and melon trio 255
  peach, Bramley and grape juice 38
  peach and Cox's juice 35
  ricotta with apple and walnuts 83
  spiced Bramleys in grape juice 192
  strawberry and apple juice 29
Aubergine fiesta 175
Avocado
  tuna and avocado with pasta 127

B
Bacon
  radicchio, sweetcorn and spinach salad with bacon 157
  scalloped roots with bacon 149
Bake, cheesy 219
Baked apples 196
Baked fish 261
Bananas, Jamaican 194
Bean
  broad beans with courgettes and cumin 171
  tomato, kidney bean and sugar snap salad 155
Beef
  beefy vegetable soup 105
  juicy beef casserole 134
  orange and lime stir-fried beef 117
Beetroot
  celery and beetroot juice 47
Blackcurrant
  blackcurrant and pineapple juice 24
Blue cheese dressing, mushroom, sweetcorn and celery salad with 161
Bolognese sauce 136
Bouillabaisse 99
Breakfast
  healthy breakfast shake 41
  hurry breakfast shake 43
  special breakfast juice 42
Broccoli
  broccoli, sprout and apple juice 54
  carrot, mangetout and broccoli juice 72
  carrot, pear and broccoli juice 53
Brûlée, mixed fruit 202

C
Cabbage
  cabbage cocktail 64
  cabbage, tomato and apple juice 65
Carrot
  carrot, cauliflower, orange and parsnip juice 58
  carrot, celery and apple juice 52
  carrot, garlic and celery juice 66

Index

carrot, mangetout and broccoli juice 72
carrot, pineapple and cucumber juice 55
carrot, sharon fruit and parsley juice 56
carrot and tomato juice 67
ginger, carrot and apple juice with tomato 61
green pepper, carrot and sharon fruit juice 59
microwaved turnips and carrots in apple juice 169

Cashew
chicken and cashew stir-fry 109

Casserole, juicy beef 134

Cauliflower
carrot, cauliflower, orange and parsnip juice 58

Celery
carrot, celery and apple juice 52
celery and beetroot juice 47
celery and carrot juice 255
mushroom, sweetcorn and celery salad with blue cheese dressing 161
spinach, tomato and celery juice 57
tomato and celery juice 62

Cheese
cheese on toast 261
cheese and tomato sandwich 263
cheesy bake 219
citrus cheesecake 208
cottage cheese pockets 85
mushroom, sweetcorn and celery salad with blue cheese dressing 161
vegetable purée with cheese 179

Cheesecake, citrus 208

Cherry
nectarine, kiwi and cherry juice 31

Chicken
chicken and cashew stir-fry 109
chicken parcels in tomato sauce 142
chicken pitta 215
chicken in plum and orange sauce 138
chicken and walnuts in grape sauce 111
classic coq au vin 140
gammon and chicken stir-fry 113
glazed chicken 220

Chinese-style, turkey 144

Choux ring with mango and strawberries 206

Chowder, haddock and sweetcorn 241

Classic coq au vin 140

Cod steaks in lime marinade 133

Coleslaw, slimmers' 167

Cottage cheese pockets 85

Courgette
broad beans with courgettes and cumin 171

Creamy jackets with tuna 97

Crispy salad with lemon and tarragon dressing 163

Cucumber
carrot, pineapple and cucumber juice 55
tomato, cucumber and pepper juice 68
tomato, melon and cucumber juice 73

Cumin
broad beans with courgettes and cumin 171

D

Desserts
baked apples 196
blackcurrant and strawberry sorbet 184

Desserts *(continued)*
  choux ring with mango and strawberries 206
  citrus cheesecake 208
  fresh fruits with Grand Marnier 189
  fromage frais fool 187
  ice cream shake 183
  Jamaican bananas 194
  lemony apple snow 188
  mango fool with strawberries 186
  melon cocktail 201
  mixed fruit brûlée 202
  pears with fruity sauce 199
  red fruit salad 191
  spiced Bramleys in grape juice 192
Diet plan recipes
  baked fish 261
  carrot and orange juice 255
  celery and carrot juice 255
  cheese on toast 261
  cheese and tomato sandwich 263
  cheesy bake 219
  chicken pitta 215
  coronation chicken sandwich 250
  fruit juice special 254
  glazed chicken 220
  haddock and sweetcorn chowder 241
  ham sandwich 261
  herb and tomato omelette 221
  mango and apple juice with grapes 256
  Mexican salad 214
  onion soup 239
  orange, apple and melon trio 255
  pasta with lentils and mushrooms 233
  pasta salad 235
  prawn salad 221
  smoked salmon open sandwich 223
  Spanish salad 242
  tomato soup 241
Dill
  halibut with dill and parsley sauce 129
Dressings
  crispy salad with lemon and tarragon dressing 163
  melon with prawns and strawberry dressing 89
  mushroom, sweetcorn and celery salad with blue cheese dressing 161

E
Eggs with mushrooms and tomatoes 95

F
Fennel
  spinach, carrot and fennel juice 69
Fish
  baked fish 261
  bouillabaisse 99
  cod steaks in lime marinade 133
  creamy jackets with tuna 97
  haddock and sweetcorn chowder 241
  halibut with dill and parsley sauce 129
  marinated salmon 131
  melon with prawns and strawberry dressing 89
  mixed seafood salad 93
  prawn provençale 122
  prawn salad 221
  smoked salmon open sandwich 223
  smoked salmon and prawns with lump fish roe and yoghurt 91
  smoked trout salad 87

Index

Fish (*continued*)
   tuna and avocado with pasta 127
Fool
   fromage frais fool 187
   mango fool with strawberries 186
Fromage frais fool 187
Fruit juices
   apple and orange juice 21
   apple and pear juice 28
   blackcurrant and pineapple shake 24
   carrot and orange juice 255
   fruit juice special 254
   fruit sunburst 18
   fruity cocktail 37
   healthy breakfast shake 41
   hurry breakfast shake 43
   kiwi, grape and melon juice 20
   mango and tangerine juice 30
   melon, orange and grapefruit trio 40
   melon, raspberry and grape juice 19
   melon solo 27
   nectarine, kiwi and cherry juice 31
   orange, lime and grape juice 26
   orange and pear juice 22
   peach, Bramley and grape juice 38
   peach and Cox's juice 35
   pineapple and satsuma juice 36
   pink grapefruit and kiwi juice 25
   plum, raspberry and grape juice 33
   satsuma and melon juice 23
   sharon fruit and melon juice 34
   special breakfast juice 42
   strawberry and apple juice 29
   strawberry cooler 32
   tangerine, pineapple and melon juice 39
   tangerine and sharon fruit juice 17
Fruity salad 159
Fruity snack 79

G
Garlic
   carrot, garlic and celery juice 66
Ginger
   marinated leg of lamb with ginger 145
Glazed chicken 220
Glazed vegetable medley 173
Grand Marnier, fresh fruits with 189
Grape
   chicken and walnuts in grape sauce 111
   melon, raspberry and grape juice 19
   orange, lime and grape juice 26
   peach, Bramley and grape juice 38
   plum, raspberry and grape juice 33
   spiced Bramleys in grape juice 192
Grapefruit
   melon, orange and grapefruit trio 40
   pink grapefruit and kiwi juice 25

H
Haddock and sweetcorn chowder 241
Halibut with dill and parsley sauce 129
Ham sandwich 261
Healthy breakfast shake 41
Herb and tomato omelette 221
Herby omelette with mushrooms 151
Homemade fruity muesli 77
Hurry breakfast shake 43

Index

I
Ice cream shake 183

J
Jamaican bananas 194
Juicy beef casserole 134

K
Kidney bean
  tomato, kidney bean and sugar snap salad 155
Kiwi
  kiwi, grape and melon juice 20
  nectarine, kiwi and cherry juice 31
  pink grapefruit and kiwi juice 25

L
Lamb
  lamb with pears 147
  marinated leg of lamb with ginger 145
Lemony apple snow 188
Lentil
  lentil and tomato soup 103
  pasta with lentils and mushrooms 233
Lime
  cod steaks in lime marinade 133
  orange, lime and grape juice 26
  orange and lime stir-fried beef 117
Lump fish roe
  smoked salmon and prawns with lump fish roe and yoghurt 91

M
Main meals
  bolognese sauce 136
  chicken parcels in tomato sauce 142
  chicken in plum and orange sauce 138
  classic coq au vin 140
  cod steaks in lime marinade 133
  halibut with dill and parsley sauce 129
  herby omelette with mushrooms 151
  juicy beef casserole 134
  lamb with pears 147
  marinated leg of lamb with ginger 145
  scalloped roots with bacon 149
  tuna and avocado with pasta 127
  turkey Chinese-style 144
Mangetout
  carrot, mangetout and broccoli juice 72
Mango
  choux ring with mango and strawberries 206
  mango and apple juice with grapes 256
  mango fool with strawberries 186
  mango and tangerine juice 30
Marinated leg of lamb with ginger 145
Marinated salmon 131
Melon
  kiwi, grape and melon juice 20
  melon cocktail 201
  melon, orange and grapefruit trio 40
  melon with prawns and strawberry dressing 89
  melon, raspberry and grape juice 19
  melon solo 27
  melon with strawberries 198
  orange, apple and melon trio 255
  satsuma and melon juice 23
  sharon fruit and melon juice 34
  tangerine, pineapple and melon juice 39
  tomato, melon and cucumber juice 73

Mexican salad 214
Microwaved turnips and carrots in apple juice 169
Mixed fruit brûlée 202
Mixed seafood salad 93
Muesli, homemade fruity 77
Mushroom
  eggs with mushrooms and tomatoes 95
  herby omelette with mushrooms 151
  mushroom, sweetcorn and celery salad with blue cheese dressing 161
  pasta with lentils and mushrooms 233

N
Nectarine
  nectarine, kiwi and cherry juice 31
Nutty vegetable stir-fry 120

O
Omelette
  herb and tomato omelette 221
  herby omelette with mushrooms 151
Onion
  onion soup 239
  tomato and onion side salad 269
Open sandwich, smoked salmon 223
Orange
  apple and orange juice 21
  carrot, cauliflower, orange and parsnip juice 58
  chicken in plum and orange sauce 138
  melon, orange and grapefruit trio 40
  orange, apple and melon trio 255
  orange, lime and grape juice 26
  orange and lime stir-fried beef 117
  orange and pear juice 22
  swede and orange purée 177
Oriental juice 50
Oriental stir-fry 115

P
Parsley
  carrot, sharon fruit and parsley juice 56
  halibut with dill and parsley sauce 129
Parsnip
  carrot, cauliflower, orange and parsnip juice 58
Pasta
  pasta with lentils and mushrooms 233
  pasta salad 235
  tuna and avocado with pasta 127
Peach
  peach, Bramley and grape juice 38
  peach and Cox's juice 35
Pear
  apple and pear juice 28
  carrot, pear and broccoli juice 53
  orange and pear juice 22
  pears with fruity sauce 199
Pepper
  green pepper, carrot and sharon fruit juice 59
  tomato, cucumber and pepper juice 68
Pineapple
  blackcurrant and pineapple shake 24
  carrot, pineapple and cucumber juice 55
  pineapple salad juice 51
  pineapple and satsuma juice 36

Pineapple *(continued)*
  tangerine, pineapple and melon juice 39
Pink grapefruit and kiwi juice 25
Pitta, chicken 215
Plum
  chicken in plum and orange sauce 138
  plum, raspberry and grape juice 33
Prawn
  melon with prawns and strawberry dressing 89
  prawn provençale 122
  prawn salad 221
  smoked salmon and prawns with lump fish roe and yoghurt 91
Purée
  swede and orange purée 177
  vegetable purée with cheese 179

R
Radicchio, sweetcorn and spinach salad with bacon 157
Raspberry
  melon, raspberry and grape juice 19
  plum, raspberry and grape juice 33
Red fruit salad 191
Reviving juice 48
Rice salad, special 165
Ricotta with apple and walnuts 83

S
Salads
  crispy salad with lemon and tarragon dressing 163
  fruity salad 159
  Mexican salad 214
  mixed seafood salad 93
  mushroom, sweetcorn and celery salad with blue cheese dressing 161
  pasta salad 235
  pineapple salad juice 51
  prawn salad 221
  radicchio, sweetcorn and spinach salad with bacon 157
  salad juice 1 70
  salad juice 2 71
  smoked trout salad 87
  Spanish salad 242
  special rice salad 165
  tomato, kidney bean and sugar snap salad 155
  tomato and onion side salad 269
Salmon
  marinated salmon 131
  smoked salmon open sandwich 233
  smoked salmon and prawns with lump fish roe and yoghurt 91
Sandwiches
  cheese and tomato sandwich 263
  coronation chicken sandwich 250
  ham sandwich 261
  smoked salmon open sandwich 223
Satsuma
  pineapple and satsuma juice 36
  satsuma and melon juice 23
Sauces
  bolognese sauce 136
  chicken parcels in tomato sauce 142
  chicken in plum and orange sauce 138
  chicken and walnuts in grape sauce 111
  halibut with dill and parsley sauce 129
  pears with fruity sauce 199
Sauté, vegetable 118
Scalloped roots with bacon 149

Index

Seafood
  mixed seafood salad 93
Shakes
  blackcurrant and pineapple shake 24
  healthy breakfast shake 41
  hurry breakfast shake 43
  ice cream shake 183
Sharon fruit
  carrot, sharon fruit and parsley juice 56
  green pepper, carrots and sharon fruit juice 59
  sharon fruit and melon juice 34
  tangerine and sharon fruit juice 17
Side salad, tomato and onion 269
Slimmers' coleslaw 167
Slimmers' trifle 204
Smoked salmon
  smoked salmon open sandwich 223
  smoked salmon and prawns with lump fish roe and yoghurt 91
Smoked trout salad 87
Snacks
  beefy vegetable soup 105
  bouillabaisse 99
  cottage cheese pockets 85
  creamy jackets with tuna 97
  eggs with mushrooms and tomatoes 95
  fruity snack 79
  homemade fruity muesli 77
  lentil and tomato soup 103
  melon with prawns and strawberry dressing 89
  Mexican salad 81
  mixed seafood salad 93
  ricotta with apple and walnuts 83
  smoked salmon and prawns with lump fish roe and yoghurt 91
  smoked trout salad 87
  vegetable soup 101
Snow, lemony apple 188
Solo, melon 27
Solo, tomato 49
Sorbet, blackcurrant and strawberry 184
Soups
  beefy vegetable soup 105
  bouillabaisse 99
  haddock and sweetcorn chowder 241
  lentil and tomato soup 103
  onion soup 239
  vegetable soup 101
Spiced Bramleys in grape juice 192
Spinach
  radicchio, sweetcorn and spinach salad with bacon 157
  spinach, tomato and celery juice 57
Spring vegetable tonic 63
Sprout
  broccoli, sprout and apple juice 54
Starters
  beefy vegetable soup 105
  bouillabaisse 99
  cottage cheese pockets 85
  eggs with mushrooms and tomatoes 95
  lentil and tomato soup 103
  melon with prawns and strawberry dressing 89
  Mexican salad 81
  mixed seafood salad 93
  ricotta with apple and walnuts 83
  smoked salmon and prawns with lump fish roe and yoghurt 91
  smoked trout salad 87
  vegetable soup 101

Index

Stir-fries
  chicken and cashew stir-fry 109
  chicken and walnuts in grape sauce 111
  gammon and chicken stir-fry 113
  marinated salmon 131
  nutty vegetable stir-fry 120
  orange and lime stir-fried beef 117
  oriental stir-fry 115
  vegetable sauté 119
Strawberry
  blackcurrant and strawberry sorbet 184
  choux ring with mango and strawberries 206
  mango fool with strawberries 186
  melon with prawns and strawberry dressing 89
  melon with strawberries 198
  strawberry and apple juice 29
  strawberry cooler 32
Sugar snap
  tomato, kidney bean and sugar snap salad 155
Sunburst, fruit 18
Swede and orange purée 177
Sweetcorn
  haddock and sweetcorn chowder 241
  mushroom, sweetcorn and celery salad with blue cheese dressing 161
  radicchio, sweetcorn and celery salad 157

T
Tangerine
  mango and tangerine juice 30
  tangerine, pineapple and melon juice 39
  tangerine and sharon fruit juice 17
Tarragon
  crispy salad with lemon and tarragon dressing 163
Toast, cheese on 261
Tomato
  cabbage, tomato and apple juice 65
  carrot and tomato juice 67
  cheese and tomato sandwich 263
  chicken parcels in tomato sauce 142
  eggs with mushrooms and tomatoes 95
  herb and tomato omelette 221
  ginger, carrot and apple juice with tomatoes 61
  lentil and tomato soup 103
  spinach, tomato and celery juice 57
  tomato and celery juice 62
  tomato, cucumber and pepper juice 68
  tomato, kidney bean and sugar snap salad 155
  tomato, melon and cucumber juice 73
  tomato and onion side salad 269
  tomato solo 49
Trifle, slimmers' 204
Tuna
  creamy jackets with tuna 97
  tuna and avocado with pasta 127
Turkey Chinese-style 144
Turnip
  microwaved turnips and carrots in apple juice 169

V
Vegetable
  beefy vegetable soup 105
  glazed vegetable medley 173
  nutty vegetable stir-fry 120
  spring vegetable tonic 63

Vegetable (*continued*)
   vegetable purée with cheese 179
   vegetable sauté 119
   vegetable soup 101

Vegetable juices
   broccoli, sprout and apple juice 54
   cabbage cocktail 64
   cabbage, tomato and apple juice 65
   carrot, cauliflower, orange and parsnip juice 58
   carrot, celery and apple juice 52
   carrot, garlic and celery juice 66
   carrot, mangetout and broccoli juice 72
   carrot and orange juice 255
   carrot, pear and broccoli juice 53
   carrot, pineapple and cucumber juice 55
   carrot, sharon fruit and parsley juice 56
   carrot and tomato juice 67
   celery and beetroot juice 47
   ginger, carrot and apple juice with tomato 61
   green pepper, carrot and sharon fruit juice 59
   oriental juice 50
   pineapple salad juice 51
   reviving juice 48
   salad juice 1 70
   salad juice 2 71
   spinach, carrot and fennel juice 69
   spinach, tomato and celery juice 57
   spring vegetable tonic 63
   tomato and celery juice 62
   tomato, cucumber and pepper juice 68
   tomato, melon and cucumber juice 73
   tomato solo 49
   vegetable medley with apple juice 60

W
Walnut
   chicken and walnuts in grape sauce 111
   ricotta with apple and walnuts 83

Y
Yoghurt
   smoked salmon and prawns with lump fish roe and yoghurt 91